Lauren

Thank you for all your
help in creating this book.
You are a joy to work with.
and I wish you much success
and happiness.

Vivian Kotha Dawson

June 17, 2009

like a weed

a
memoir

by
vivian kostka dawson

A coming of age story of a Hungarian girl
through WWII and the post war years as a Displaced Person.

authorHOUSE®

AuthorHouse™
1663 Liberty Drive, Suite 200
Bloomington, IN 47403
www.authorhouse.com
Phone: 1-800-839-8640

First published by AuthorHouse 2/23/2009

ISBN: 978-1-4389-4694-8 (sc)
ISBN: 978-1-4389-4695-5 (hc)

Library of Congress Control Number: 2009900262

Printed in the United States of America
Bloomington, Indiana

This book is printed on acid-free paper.

Cover design by Veronika Hargis.

for my mother

Old House

I was born on April 19, 1933. The first eleven years of my life I lived in a big beautiful house in the middle of a big beautiful garden in the woodsy, hilly outskirts of Budapest, Hungary. The house was built in the first decade of the 20th century by my grandparents. My mother was a little girl when the house was ready to be lived in. Her two brothers were born soon afterward. In my time, the people who lived in the house were my grandparents, their older son (my Uncle George), my beautiful, recently widowed mother Vera, and our beloved nanny, who by then was gnarled by arthritis but still managed to lovingly care for me. She occupied that space between family and servants delegated to governesses, tutors, and nannies, always wore an apron much like a jumper over her dress, liked her solitude, and often took her meals by herself.

For a while we had a parade of young women to help with the cooking and to keep the house clean, but until the day a cheerful, lively, rotund country girl came to apply, none was found suitable. Kati was immediately loved by all. She did take a rather casual approach toward dusting, polishing, and housework in general, but her meals were magnificent productions, and the whole family was thoroughly delighted. Our famous Sunday dinners, taken around two in the afternoon, became the highlight of family life. To this day, what I know about the art of cooking came from watching Kati work her magic while I stood on a chair next to the stove in the big blue and white steaming kitchen, with all its shining copper pots and pans. The house itself was a two-storied affair, sturdily built, with attic and cellar. A servant couple lived with their little girl in a small apartment in the semi-basement. The man was more or less a watchman, a gardener, and an all-around handyman, but not much visible work resulted. His wife, a quiet, skinny little woman, helped with routine household chores. Their daughter Veti, the same age as I, became my lifelong best friend even though we had, in the beginning, several hair-pulling episodes.

I should mention that my father died of peritonitis when I was six months old. He was forty-nine. It was very sudden. My mother told how on a Friday they went to the movies and the funeral was next Tuesday. After a while, my mother went to work as some sort of secretary to the head of a big governmental judicial office in the city. She said she never learned to type with more than two fingers, but the job paid a lot more than teaching school, which she was trained for. I daresay the prospect of working with all those young prosecutors and law clerks may have had something to do with her decision as well. She eventually did marry one of the bright young lawyers.

There was no question that the world in this big beautiful place was a matriarchy. My grandmother ruled with a loving but iron hand. I really think everyone, with the possible exception of my grandfather, was just a little bit afraid of her, but one could never say why. She breakfasted around ten at the dining room table amidst a steaming pot of tea nestled under a large embroidered tea cozy with a pompom, croissants and brioches, and jam made with fruits from the garden, taking her time. She read the newspaper from first page to last. By this time, she was fully dressed and the household accounts, her extensive correspondence, and her instructions and plans had all been taken care of. I had no idea of all this, of course. I took it for granted that everything was always as it should be in the house.

I was equally comfortable with the men and women in my circle, an attitude I maintained throughout my life and one that served me very well. I suppose I owe this to my relationship with my grandfather, who was my best friend, particularly in the early years of my childhood. One of our chores was to set the midday meal table. It was covered already with a white damask tablecloth, then a smaller one in the center, usually edged with lace and embroidery but always all white. I learned where the fork went, the knife and the soup spoon, the wine and water glasses next to each other, the large everyday plate with the gold and blue edge and the soup plate on top of it. Next to my grandfather's chair, he put a round tray with both red and white wine, a large green bottle of mineral water, and two small canisters—one with oil, one with vinegar. He made the vinegar himself in the upstairs bathroom from leftover wine. A cabinet was filled with medicine bottles holding vinegars of all ages and colors. Some were truly awful, some delicious. I chattered away while we worked and he listened with a bemused expression, his eyes smiling. I have a sepia photo of him where this expression is memorialized. For a long time, whenever I looked at it, he appeared exactly as I knew him. With time, both the picture and my memory have faded.

He and I went for frequent short walks in the neighborhood, often with some destination; some as mundane as the mailbox, some as exotic as the pharmacy where glassed double doors rang the bell above to announce our arrival. It was a magical place of black and white tiles, chrome handled glass cabinets, and shelves of narrow necked bottles. From behind the counter, the pharmacists greeted with deference the distinguished old doctor and his little granddaughter. Evidently, I had grown since the last visit. After a mysterious professional discourse, followed by the purchase, we said our cordial goodbyes and walked home. I felt tall.

When grandmother joined us, we took outings. These were long walks in the large nearby woods. Fall was particularly lovely. My grandparents had matching loden capes with woven leather buttons they had bought in Austria. Whatever they bought was of top quality, but it was meant to last forever. They both had walking sticks. Nowadays walking sticks usually denote some sort of infirmity, but in those days they were a necessary accessory.

Once a year, these excursions took us to the cemetery where family members were buried. This was my annual visit to my father. Another grave that was given special attention was that of my grandparents' youngest child, Michael, who died just two years before my entry into the world. We cleaned the graves of fallen leaves and debris, put fresh flowers on them, and sometimes my grandmother told stories of the people buried there. Then, as in the woods, we had the "piknik." This consisted of hard boiled eggs for sure, and some rolls; not much but infinitely delicious. On rare occasions, my mother joined the three of us for a walk in the woods. It made me happy.

I adored my mother. We did a lot of interesting things together. Government office hours were from eight in the morning until two in the afternoon. So unless Mommy stayed in the city, she often had women friends in for tea. When I was very little, I was sometimes jealous of these people who took from my playtime, and I let them know it. I was known to march into the room, sit down, cross my arms, and stare at her guest. One lady actually ran out of the house, exclaiming, "I cannot take any more of this!" Both she and my mother told the story many times with peals of laughter. As I got older, I began to enjoy the company of her friends, and even joined the conversations. I spent most of my time in the company of adults and I imitated their way of speaking. I was about five when one of her friends asked me if I had a cold since I blew my nose several times and held a handkerchief in my hand all afternoon. "Please make a note to yourself," I replied archly, "I always have a cold." My mother and others as well began to tell these and many more stories. Pretty soon they became part of the family lore. I took all this attention with aplomb. Once, as an adult, I asked Mommy what I was like in those days. She tilted her head to the side, cupped my chin in her hands, and said ever so tenderly, "Oh my dear, you were such a darling, clever little thing".

I can to this day viscerally recall how majestic those woods were, how magical the wild flowered meadows, how elegant the tree-lined road to the pharmacy. I can see the sunlight dancing on my grandfather's vinegar bottles from the vantage point of my white porcelain chamber pot, and feel what it was to be so loved and so safe when I was a clever little girl.

The Garden

When I wasn't otherwise occupied, I spent most of my time in the garden. I knew every inch of it. In the front of the house, a formal garden was kept with an immaculately manicured oval lawn, on one corner of which stood an enormous horse chestnut tree. One could take refuge under it during a summer rain. Often in summer evenings, supper was taken here on a white wooden table. My mother always had a large bottle of English Lavender eau de cologne to keep the mosquitoes away. I don't actually remember that it worked, but I liked the scent. Nearby, a round, formal flowerbed glowed with all colors of magnificent tulips in the spring, and red geraniums throughout the summer. In the winter, it was covered with snow, as was everything else in the garden.

The rest of the garden was in a more natural state. A path along a row of currant and rose bushes led to the small swimming pool in the far end of the property. There were plenty of fruit trees: cherry, plum, peach, apricot, apple, pear, and one exotic quince, plus a majestic walnut tree and a slender hazelnut bush. The vegetable garden was partially hidden by a flowerbed border. Groves of trees, each unique, some for hiding, some for climbing, and two wild flowered meadows to walk in the tall grass in the summer haze. The melodic humming of friendly insects for background music where a little girl's imaginations could soar and take her to exotic, magical places. When reading became my favorite pastime, I often spent hours in one of the upper branches of a pine tree. I was mostly alone, but never lonely there. This place that now exists only in my imagination is where I still go for solace, to gather my thoughts, to find peace. Gregarious as I turned out to be, I still need that solitude that my garden taught me to cherish.

When the grass got too tall, a Swabian man from a nearby village, one of my grandmother's army of experts, came and cut it with large, rhythmic swings of his scythe. In the spring he was the one who tilled the vegetable garden and the flowerbeds. He wore wide-wale corduroy pants, criss-cross suspenders, and a leather cap with a visor. The fallen grass was allowed to dry, then gathered into stacks. The temptation to jump into the soft and inviting haystacks was impossible to resist. Veti and I would climb on the top, then roll or slide down, throwing bunches of the fragrant hay at each other. But, alas, we were told the animals don't like it if it's been trampled on by humans, so after that, we had to content ourselves with languishing lazily at the foot of the stack and gazing up at the mellowing summer sky. After a suitable time, the Swabian man came back with a large, horse-drawn wagon and took away his golden bounty.

Toward the middle of September, the leaves began to turn. Soon, the garden as well as the surrounding hills glowed with an array of gold and orange leaves, like flames, in the fading sun. Usually, by late October the trees were all bare. So much fun to run in the thick carpet of dry leaves, to gather them in front of the swing, get up real high, and jump into the pile with wild abandon. Less fun to put them in large piles. It was hard work. Then the piles were burned and the garden was dotted with pyres. The sky was already a dark gray. The three of us—my grandmother, the gardener, and I—worked silently in the bone chilling cold. She put some potatoes in the embers of one of the fires. When they were done, we pulled them out with a rake and allowed them to cool before we ate them as we stood around the fire. Infinitely satisfying. In the meantime, the fires burned themselves out. We had to make sure nothing was smoldering before we returned to the house.

For a while, it seemed as though the garden, drained of all color under the ever-darkening sky, stood still in time, expectant. Then one morning, my bedroom was bathed in a filtered white light. The snow had arrived, and it came to stay.

I have never had to deal with snow as an adult. I just remember how enjoyable my childhood winters were. When I was very little, someone, usually my mother, would pull me on a little sled, or I would sit in someone's lap to glide down the small slope in our own garden. Soon I graduated to the much steeper meadow just across the dirt road that led to the woods. I became a solo sledder, then eventually I tried my mother's skis. That was very difficult, but then a size-appropriate set arrived and I thus began practicing this great sport in earnest. Veti wasn't that delighted and soon tired of the cold. But there were always other kids from the neighborhood. My particular friends were the brothers Attila and Matthew. They were named after great Hungarian heroes, one for the Great Hun, of course, and the other for the Great Renaissance King of Hungary. Attila was a classmate of mine at the neighborhood elementary school. We usually walked home together with little Matthew tagging along. Once home, we just had time to eat a hurried meal, put on our gear, and hit the slope.

One day somebody got the great idea of building a ski jump. It was a magnificent feat of engineering. We packed the snow against the concrete railing that separated the road from the meadow so it was much higher than the ground, then we kept packing it until we got a good launching pad and made the whole thing concave so that we ended up high enough at the jumping off point that we actually had a good lift. I had never seen ski jumping. I cannot remember what form we used. All I know is that it was exhilarating to fly through the air, if even for a few seconds. Only the fading light would bring me back to the house. I had to practically thaw out. On one occasion, I tried warming my icy feet against the ceramic-tiled stove in the upstairs library. This, of course, caused an incredible, throbbing pain in my toes. I remember rocking back and forth, my fingers wrapped around the offending digits, trying not to cry out loud because my grandmother had guests for tea in the next room. To this day, whenever I am in snow or ice, my big toes begin to ache.

Downstairs

Buddhists say the only constant in life is change. And so it was with the villa. Back when my mother and father got married, the house was radically remodeled into two apartments, but so closely connected that it retained its character as one home. Another kitchen was added upstairs and what was a powder room on the first floor was enlarged and redesigned as a full bathroom. The original house had a grand entry hall two stories high with a curved staircase. It must have been quite a feat to horizontally separate it into two: the downstairs library and my grandparents' dayroom upstairs. The staircase was eliminated and the back stairs were upgraded with carpeting and a carved walnut railing.

My first memories are of my mother and I living downstairs, with the upstairs being the apartments of my grandparents and nanny. Essentially the downstairs had three living areas interconnected by tall double doors. My mother's and my bedroom was square with tall French windows that looked out toward the round manicured lawn. While all the rest of the house had massive dark furniture, most of it from the nineteenth century, this room was furnished with a delicate, inlaid rosewood Art Deco bedroom set chosen by my parents. The walls were decorated with pink roses, each one painted carefully by hand by a craftsman I followed around, marveling at his artistry. I slept on a daybed set against the wall opposite the foot of my mother's bed. I have a picture in my mind of fluttering lace curtains at the open window while the climbing roses from the outside wall peek into the room at my sleeping mother, her mop of hair sticking out from under the celadon colored, jacquard duvet.

These were happy days. Slowly my mother recovered from her mourning. The black dresses gave way to color, mostly pale blues, her favorite. She had a lovely, trained voice, and she'd go about the house singing. She went out more often, sometimes staying in town after work and sometimes donning formal gowns and leaving for the evening. At first, I loudly protested, so Mommy took to going to bed at the same time as I, and then sneaking out once I was sound asleep. Mercifully for both of us, I never woke up to find her bed empty. I was all grown up when

Mommy told me about this dangerous deception and by that time it was only another charming memory we shared.

The rectangular dining hall that faced the same way as our bedroom was used only for the infrequent dinner parties. I only remember the long table, the chairs, and the piano, but I know it had other furniture as well. The parquet floor was covered with a large, boldly colored Oriental rug. All the rooms had the same type of floor and were strewn with somewhat faded rugs known generically as the Persians. Some were quite worn and had been in the family for generations. The east end of the dining hall had square-paned double doors, also in the French style, that opened onto the terrace where I spent my first summer in my pram gazing up at the dancing leaves of an old white ash tree.

One day my uncle brought home a wife and the family dining room became their living quarters. My new aunt Valeria could have been called exotic with her chiseled strong face; her nose, though not unattractive was beaklike, her hair jet black. She owned a combination gallery and shop of Hungarian folk art in which she was an expert. When later I had occasion to be in school productions with ethnic themes, she would lend me beautiful authentic costumes to wear. But there was an edge to her that I sensed even as a little girl.

Most of what happened in my life took place in the downstairs library. The windows here had a northern exposure and looked out onto the great meadow of the ski jump. One entered through an anteroom from the west, which faced the wide, paved street, where Number 83 of the famous yellow Budapest streetcars ran. It was the lifeline of our neighborhood known as *Huvosvolgy*— Cool Valley in English.

One wall of the library was completely given to bookcases and a built-in, comforting sofa upholstered in green corduroy. Before I knew how to read, I spent hours with the large art books from the bottom shelves. I learned about Adam and Eve, and Napoleon, in royal velvet, crowning himself or riding a fierce steed to victory; Venus, with wind-blown hair emerging, demurely naked, from the sea; the Spanish Royal Family accompanied by dogs and dwarfs; and many other wondrous things. As a young couple, my grandparents traveled throughout Europe and often bought books in museums. Years later, whenever I visited places such as the Louvre, the Uffizi, or the Prado, it was as though I were walking through the books of my childhood.

The Boy with the Golden Hair

Another important person in my life was my half brother. Unfortunately, he played a peripheral role in my daily life, but his visits were wonderful for me. He was the issue of my father's previous marriage. I say previous because there seemed to have been a first wife, but the whole affair was as shrouded in mystery as most of my father's life. Even some family members didn't know this, but my mother had a painted photograph of an aristocratic English lady in a lacy, high-collared dress and large brimmed hat with flowery excess so popular with Edwardian ladies. My father's and her story is so classic that one can hear the opening bars of the music from "Masterpiece Theatre." Evidently my father, Istvan Kostka, a young, dashing hussar (I have a photo of him to prove it), was on assignment as part of a retinue of a dignitary to London. There at some waltzy evening, he met the beautiful daughter of Sir and Lady Somebody and they fell in love. Sounds a bit like a comic opera by Lehar, but it's true. They eloped. The family was aghast, and the ill-fated marriage was annulled.

Then life got a little darker for Europe, and for my father, as the nightmare we now call World War I commenced. Istvan Kostka was still dashing, but now he was a cavalry officer on the Russian front on a horse.

Among his things I found some letter from a silly, flirty young girl full of teasings and descriptions of her adventures at fashionable watering places throughout the Austro-Hungarian Empire. My father must have found them charming, because when the war was over, he married her. They had a son, my beautiful golden brother Zdenko Harald.

Evidently, the young lady's fancy for young officers was not abated by marriage or motherhood, for she still enjoyed their company. One stood out, as one inevitably always does. One day my father returned from a business trip from London and he called home from the train station. Telephones in those days were a little unpredictable and he accidentally got in on the party line and overheard his wife arrange an assignation with a young lieutenant. Father was still an officer; he still had a sword, but now also carried a sidearm. So did the young unsuspecting lieutenant who was no doubt looking forward to a delightful afternoon with his charming companion when he came face to face with her husband, my father, as he rounded a corner. What happened next no one knows. Lawyers and courts battled it out for years. But the one thing that was certain is that the young officer was shot and taken to the hospital, where he died. Was it a duel? Was it murder? Did the young officer reach for his gun? My father was arrested but continued to maintain throughout his life that he had acted honorably in the matter. It was a big scandal of course. Newspapers were full of the details. I've read some trial transcripts—mostly the vilifying testimony of a maid to my brother's mother. The same paparazzi that followed the Prince of Wales and that Simpson woman a few years later made mincemeat of everyone's reputation. My brother went to live with a maiden aunt, his grandparents being dead, his father in prison for manslaughter, and his mother not wanting or not being able to take him.

It was years later that my mother met my father. After his release from prison, Istvan rented a small guesthouse of a villa just a few houses down from our house. My mother told of a fairy tale romance—their first meeting, courtship, and eventual marriage. Needless to say, my grandfather was not absolutely delighted, but our family being as they were opened their house, as well as their hearts, to the new additions to the family. This is when the remodeling of the house came about.

I daresay the next few short years that my brother spent in the relative calm and loving atmosphere of his new home were the happiest in his entire life. He said as much himself to me years later. He was eleven when he moved in and thirteen when our father died and he was obliged to move back with his aunt again.

Of course, I don't remember any of this or the subsequent few years. Once I was able to communicate and relate, Zdenko often visited and played with me with obvious enjoyment. He carried me on his shoulders on walks in the woods, went swimming with me, and taught me games, my favorite of which was with his favorite: Napoleonic-uniformed lead toy soldiers. We called it our Austerlitz game and to this day I know how that battle was fought; it was the one that got me interested in Waterloo and much later, Gettysburg.

Zdenko was charming, funny, lively, and told amusing stories that may or may not have been true, and he was never for a moment boring. I adored my brother of the golden hair. He took my favorite photograph of myself in the summer of 1944 when he came in the uniform of an army private to say goodbye.

Art

As a little girl, I was surrounded by paintings that were created mostly by ancestors or relatives. Paintings were very important in the family. My grandfather's grandfather, Miklos Barabas, was a well-known artist most famous for the portraits he did of political figures, artists, and other luminaries. He studied abroad in Italy and France, where he fell in love and married my great-great grandmother. Several portraits of her, himself, as well as those of other family members, drawings, plus some beautiful watercolors of Italy, covered the walls of the old house. His autobiography, a marvelous depiction of eighteenth century life, was readied for publication by my grandmother. The photographer who came to the house chose the upstairs dining room for the best light to set up his camera equipment. The paintings were brought in one by one and placed on an easel at the appropriate angle to the incoming sunlight. When he allowed me to look through the lens, I discovered with delight that the pictures appeared upside down. It was exciting when the beautifully finished books finally arrived. My grandfather inscribed one of the first ones to me. It remains one of my greatest treasures.

The downstairs library had two very large landscapes by another artist, Tivadar Csontvary-Kostka, who was related to me on my father's side. Today he is considered one of the most important modern artists. A museum dedicated to his work is in the town called Pecs in southwestern Hungary. Other works of his are in the National Gallery in Budapest, and many are in Israel. As much as I loved all the pictures in the house, I felt that while the Barabas portraits and landscapes belonged to everyone in the house, the Csontvary-Kostka paintings were Zdenko's and my special legacies from our father.

Books

Although I understood, more or less, and appreciated the intrinsic, esthetic value of the visual arts, I was more captivated by the beauty of the written word. I took to reading like a duck to water, so to speak.

Although I was pretty average in other subjects, I soon outstripped the other students in reading. I was slightly obsessed in the beginning. Riding on the streetcar, I read every sign, every advertisement, whatever writing appeared in shop windows, and all the rules and warnings that came my way. At home, of course, I read books. Because I liked to read in bed before going to sleep, I was given a little pale blue reading lamp with a bendable arm. Sometimes, if Mommy was bothered by the light, I would take it under the covers and read in secret.

Veti shared my enthusiasm for books, as did some of the other girls from school. Swapping them and talking about them was great fun. We didn't think it was a great cultural exercise or something to celebrate. It was, after all, a time before the advent of television, and movies were a rare and exotic phenomena.

Curiously, the first movie I ever saw was *The Invisible Man* with Claude Raines when I was in either the first or second grade. It was a school project, and a group of us marched off with a teacher to the neighborhood youth center. It took me years to figure out why we saw that particular film, so obviously inappropriate for our age group. The elementary school that we attended was named after a popular author whose best-known work was a historical novel of the last years of Attila the Hun titled *The Invisible Man*. My best guess is that some eager school maven saw that this film was to be shown and decided, without bothering to check it out, that it would be an excellent history lesson for all of us. I was totally baffled by the experience. It was years before I saw another movie, which was fine with me.

A Gentleman Comes Calling

One afternoon, instead of the customary lady friends who came to tea, a gentleman was expected. I eagerly anticipated his arrival. When the doorbell rang, I scurried out of the bedroom before the last buttons of my little white corduroy dress could be fastened. I was known for running away before I was fully dressed. Some exasperated soul usually ran after me, buttoning me up as best as they could.

It seems the gentleman came courting that afternoon. Not my mother, for, unbeknownst to me, he had already won her heart, but *moi*. Although I entered the room in haste, I hesitated and very shyly, half-hidden behind a velvet Bordeaux arm chair, peeked out at him. He was a tall, slender man, with dark hair, combed straight back in the fashion of the day, and he wore gold-framed glasses over his brown eyes. His well-cut suit was much different from the old fashioned stiff-collared formal elegance of my grandfather or the unmade bed appearance of my artistic uncle. He had a pleasant, relaxed air about him. He paid a lot of attention to me, seemed interested in what I had to say, and even took the time to play with me. I was not aware just how much was riding on my approval. Happily, according to plan, I was totally charmed.

After that he became a regular visitor. Sometimes he'd play the piano, very beautifully, with meaningful glances at my mother, asking if she remembered a particular piece. But mostly they would just get lost in conversation, or rather she'd listen with great interest while he talked. Whenever Mommy would announce that she was expecting a visitor, I would knowingly nod. "I know, it's George," I'd say with resignation.

Eventually, Mommy and George announced their intention to get married. She invited his mother, who came with his older sister, Sari, and her husband for an evening visit. My grandparents came downstairs, looking very elegant. Grandmother wore a black raw silk suit with a pleated bodice and her beautiful emerald green cloisonné pin in the shape of an oak leaf with a diamond dewdrop. Cognac, liqueurs, chocolate bonbons, and a tray of small pastries were laid out on a small table. My mother handed out demitasses of strong aromatic Turkish coffee. It was a lovely evening. Everyone was eager to please and be pleased.

My new grandmother-to-be made every effort to welcome me as one of her granddaughters and in return I admired her beautiful white hair as much as her kindness and was totally prepared to love her. She knitted me a sweater just like the ones she made for my two new cousins as a token of her intentions. My new aunt gave me a special prayer book. Suddenly, I was about to acquire a new set of relatives, and as it turned out, our destinies were to be more closely connected than with my other relations.

Shortly after Christmas in 1941, Mommy and George were married in a civil ceremony. George's mother hosted a reception for them at her city apartment, after which the newlyweds left for their honeymoon at a winter resort in the Tatra mountains in northern Hungary near the Slovak border. For the duration, I moved upstairs and slept in my grandparents' bedroom on a chaise lounge. I wrote several postcards to my mother complaining that I couldn't sleep because the old folks snored a lot.

My uncle prepared for their return by making a huge welcoming sign and a surprise party in the library. He also gave them a wonderful painting of a misty, black and white landscape of poplars in the snow. We had a lively and joyful evening that in many ways ushered in a new life in the old house.

Another George Joins the Family

Naturally there were changes after George and Mommy returned from their honeymoon. Mommy and I continued to share our bedroom and George took the smaller room that was left vacant after my poor nanny's death. Her comfortable but austere room had a different ambiance once the new occupant got done refurnishing it. A deep and comfortable daybed covered with an Oriental rug and strewn with big goose down decorative pillows took up almost half of the small room. His immense record collection was held in a cabinet with a built-in record player and shelves for books and other personal items. There was a large shaded lamp on an end table the other side of the daybed. Its amber light gave an elegant yet cozy feel to the room. I was truly impressed when I was invited to inspect the transformation. George served delicate cookies from a tin box the likes of which I never tasted and I was even allowed to wash them down with a thimble full of sweet Spanish sherry. As I liked to share everything with Veti, I invited her one afternoon when no one was around to a viewing and to taste this wondrous combination of cookies and sherry. We ended up making quite a dent in the supply and, as a consequence, got into a lot of trouble—but it was worth it.

George came with so many books that the downstairs library had to have a floor-to-ceiling bookcase built on two walls and a sliding ladder to reach the ones on the top. This room now became the focus of family gatherings. Sunday dinners would turn into afternoons of animated conversations. There was a new energy in the house. My uncle and my stepfather became instant friends, and even on weekdays their discussions would last way into the night, long after their exhausted wives retired. This arrangement pleased my mother, because she loved them both very much, but it did not sit well with Aunt Valeria. For a while, no one noticed that in addition to the imminent threat of war, a private storm was gathering amidst all the merriment in the old house.

While all this was going on, I was busy living my own life. That winter I saw my first opera, *Hansel and Gretel*, and the ballet *Copelia*, and was enchanted by both. I had school, I had the snow, I had my books, and then it hit. Suddenly my uncle and aunt distanced themselves from the rest of the family, would not allow my one-year-old cousin to see his grandparents, and Aunt Valeria tried to turn everyone—servants, my brother, even me—against George. It broke my mother's heart and George never forgave Aunt Valeria for that. I suppose this tragic fiasco was partially the cause for the decision for our leaving the old house and perhaps even the country. Nevertheless, the schism between my grandparents and Aunt Valeria's troops continued for years, way into the Communist era.

Nobody ever told me what opportunity she seized to bring about this break in the family. The primary reason that everyone agreed upon was her possessiveness and jealousy, but it is so difficult to fathom that a woman would go this far to have someone to herself and to have the ability to persuade another human being to turn against all the people he loved and who loved him.

Once the initial turmoil died down and many months before our eventual departure, life returned to an almost normal and, for me, amiable routine upstairs with my grandparents and Mommy and George. Aunt Viola continued her monthly luncheon visits and various acquaintances of the adults often came for tea or a shot of apricot brandy, usually old colleagues of my grandfather. Before the army got him, Zdenko showed up regularly, which for me always remained a treat. Veti was my constant companion—although, particularly after her father was away in the army, her mother often complained that she spent too much time upstairs and not enough with her.

On winter Sunday afternoons, the upstairs library of the old house was filled with music from the radio, interspersed with the consonance of human voices and laughter that emanates not as a response to humor but from the enjoyment and delight of the people assembled. The tea cart, pushed now to the side, still held the remains of the midday meal. My mother was busy roasting coffee beans over a votive candle in an apparatus that resembled a tiny cement mixer. When the beans were dark brown, she transferred them to a minaret-shaped grinder and from there into the copper pitcher already filled with water, bringing it to a boil over the votive flame. The final product, the richly brown Turkish coffee with consistency almost like molasses, was then finally served in demitasses. Meanwhile, George carefully poured a finger or so of Armagnac into snifters. My grandmother produced her box of Christmas bonbons of dark and bitter chocolate and offered it around. I passed on those. What I liked were the little sugar cubes soaked in coffee or brandy.

Clouds of cigarette smoke filled the room. Even my grandmother had one of her very special gold-tipped brand. She smoked one a week. I sat near the tall, ceramic stove a little away from the group, listening and observing and now and then drifting into my own thoughts. Through the curtain of the smoke and the steam from the coffees, I could see the snowy meadow dotted with the small figures of the weekend sled riders, the large bare trees, the hazy winter sky. It was more beautiful than any painting I had ever seen.

Montage of Life in the Villa

Several years passed between George's first visit and the wedding. Much was happening in the interim, both in the world at large and my life. I had long since outgrown my little white corduroy dress and been outfitted for school. In September 1939, I started first grade at our neighborhood elementary school for both boys and girls, where no uniform was required, but my new clothes very much reflected the traditional school style. I got a navy blue pleated woolen skirt, a couple of light blue polo shirts, and a jumper-like apron to protect me from ink spots. I was further outfitted with a square leather backpack and a small basket with leather straps to carry a snack for the ten o'clock break. Classes started at eight and were let out at one, Monday through Saturday. The schoolhouse was within easy walking distance from our house and for the first year or two I was always accompanied by an adult, but after that I came and went by myself, often with other kids who lived our way. During winters, the snow was piled five or six feet high between the roadbed and the wide sidewalks. Naturally, if you were a kid, you walked on top of it, stopping now and then to throw a snowball or two and get blasted in return.

School didn't turn out to be a big deal. I was a pretty good student and more or less liked my teachers until the one I had in fourth grade who obviously didn't like me, and I still remember, often too late, the warning of my third grade teacher who cautioned me about leaping before thinking. We had one teacher for all subjects each year, except for the music teacher and our religious instructor. Religious studies were required even in public schools, and the students were separated by their various faiths to be instructed by priests, ministers, and such. Religion was never an issue in the old house, but grandmother dutifully fulfilled my father's wishes that I be instructed in the Roman Catholic faith and she saw to it that I learned all my lessons. My mother would have nothing to do with it, but now and then I would try to drag her to church with me. I think I succeeded one time but eventually gave up. It never really took with me either after my initial, short-lived fervor.

There were no language classes at my school, so my mother hired a distant relative, a "lady who has fallen on hard times" by the name of Tante Tonchi, to teach me German. She came out to the house once or twice a week with her somewhat unorthodox methods of teaching. Basically, I learned a lot of fairy tales and little songs I remember to this day, but not much else. When I entered boarding school later and was enrolled in advanced classes based on the previous years' experience, it was discovered that I spoke almost no German at all. "And I paid her a fortune for this?" my mother exclaimed in exasperation.

Toward the late autumn of first grade, what started out as a cold turned into a very bad inner ear infection. The pediatrician finally decided to call in a specialist. He came to the house regularly to lance my ears. It was a very painful procedure and I put up quite a fight accompanied by ear-piercing shrieks—pun intended—to the great distress and embarrassment of my mother and the annoyance of the doctor. My head was completely bandaged with special padding on my ears, to which I added my paternal grandmother's dangling diamond earrings I found in the small leather jewelry box I was given to play with. It was just the touch my turban needed.

There was talk of a mastoidectomy, but miraculously, on the day before Christmas, my fever broke. The crisis was over. We were all very relieved and grateful. On Christmas Eve, I was carried into the library, where the floor-to-ceiling tree glowed with real candles, our beautiful old ornaments, and the special Christmas candy wrapped in fancy pink and blue pastel papers with silver or gold covers.

Most of the presents were for me. Christmas was for the children. It was the custom for grown-ups to exchange small special gifts, albeit sometimes quite expensive. My grandmother always received a beautiful cyclamen plant and a box of a very special brand of bitter, dark chocolate bonbons. I still have the small, sterling cigarette case my mother received one year.

After the lighting ceremony, my grandfather extinguished the candles with a long pole tipped by a wet sponge before we adjourned to the dining room for our traditional Christmas Eve champagne supper. I especially loved the foie gras and the pureed chestnuts with whipped cream. Throughout the next few days, the sideboard held trays of delicious baked goods there for the taking.

Shortly after New Year, my mother took some time off from work and she and I went down to a spa at Lake Balaton to get me back to good health. This very large lake is a year-round favorite, not only with Hungarians, but visitors from other countries as well. It is so big that one cannot see the other side with the naked eye. Large and small towns dot the shoreline. Some are famous resorts, others are known for their sanitariums or sport centers, and some best known for their waterfront summer homes. Towns display plaques with names of world famous people who came for the cure. Sailing is taken very seriously, and with the prevailing winds on the lake, the skills required are equal to those in the San Francisco Bay or the America's Cup races. One previous summer, we stayed with friends of my mother in their villa with a large dock from which the swimmers and boats were launched. We got to ride along on relatively easy sailing excursions. Other times, Mommy would swim for what seemed like hours with slow and elegant breaststrokes, her head out of the water, in the manner of European ladies of the period.

My grandmother also loved to swim, and she and my grandfather would spend a few days at a small bed and breakfast in early September after the noisy vacationers left. Her bathing costume was the traditional black, bloomer style with white piping, but her head was bare. My mother's, however, was made of the new stretch material that, once wet, clung closely to the body.

Lake Balaton got lively again once winter arrived. Sailing and fishing resumed in another form. The world was white, cold, crystalline, and misty. The solidly frozen lake had an ethereal ambiance, yet it was full of lively people playing on the ice and snow. I wasn't very good at skating, but really enjoyed riding on the special wooden chairs equipped with runners propelled by the rider with spiked poles. If I got enough momentum, I would glide smoothly for quite a distance. I also learned to like hotel living and eating in restaurants. Each afternoon, before tea, we spent some time in the library reading and writing. I sent postcards to my first grade teacher and my grandparents. When we got back, I was reading fluently.

In the cold rainy spring of 1940, our beloved nanny died. She had come to the service of my great-great-grandfather's family from her native Transylvania when she was only sixteen years old. Years later, she joined the household of my newly minted physician grandfather and his bride with the golden hair when they started their family with the birth of my mother. She was laid out in her small upstairs bedroom and I was allowed one last visit. I had yet to fully comprehend the finality of death and approached her more with puerile curiosity than any other emotion. She looked as she always did to me. Cook requested to come and view Nanny's remains as well. My grandparents, my mother, and I sat motionless in the upstairs library, listening to her strident wailing in accordance with the custom of her village to honor the dead. The following day, I was much more unsettled by my mother's quiet tears, and clung to her on the stairs while two men took the coffin away.

Once school let out at the end of May, I was scheduled to have my tonsils out on advice of the doctors who attended me during my illness the previous autumn. Aunt Valeria had to have hers out as well, so we shared a hospital room. I found out later that the surgeon who performed my operation had a romantic interest in my mother and that she forbade George to come and see me just in case. Sometimes my mother's logic surprised everyone; nevertheless, I did get exceptionally good care and frequent doctor visits. I came through with flying colors and was prancing around the hospital while poor Aunt Valeria was languishing in her bed of pain. But I didn't get the bicycle I was promised because the doctors forbade it.

We were all very sorry when Cook announced that she had to leave us to return to her village because her family needed her. It was to be for an indefinite but temporary period, and no one was hired to replace her.

After Kati left, our main midday meals were delivered each day by a young man on a bicycle from a nearby restaurant in pots that were designed to fit on top of one another and held together by a brace so he could carry them in one hand while guiding his bike with the other. Dessert was on the bottom, the top held the soup and so on. My grandmother re-warmed them and served them in china dishes on the table my grandfather and I set for the three of us. My grandfather's and my friendship really blossomed at this time. We shared an aperitif before each luncheon; mine was a thimbleful of liquid iron designed to bring me back to health and his was a shot glass of apricot brandy. We saluted each other before we threw them back and down our throats.

Sometime during this year, my mother and I moved upstairs so that my Uncle George and Aunt Valeria could have a proper apartment of two rooms. The downstairs library was still primarily used by my mother and me, but I began to establish new headquarters upstairs. Our new bedroom was really more mine, with a small table that served as my desk in the center, a bookcase with my collections of teddy bears on the top shelf, and a beautiful nineteenth century dollhouse that once belonged to Grandmother and her sister centered on a long cabinet that held all my toys. The window over the cabinet opened to a balcony with a view of our garden below and the woods of the Buda hills beyond. In summertime, we would often have our lunch or afternoon tea out there. On hot days,

I'd have iced coffee, with lots of milk and a drop or two of coffee. In the winter, we put seeds out for the birds over the snowy table. It was lovely watching their comings and goings against the foggy winter landscape.

Although we moved freely throughout the rooms in the house, it seemed that each of us had our very own sanctuary. My grandparents' bedroom directly over the rose-walled one we had downstairs was definitely my grandmother's domain. It was full of furniture, but didn't ever appear cluttered. The twin beds were pushed together, with nightstands on either side. Against the foot of the beds was her beautiful narrow Biedermeier desk where the business of the household was conducted, covered with neatly stacked papers, an ornate inkstand in the Rococo style, a mother-of-pearl and silver letter opener, and her leather-bound daily reminder. Next to it was her trusty old Singer sewing machine. In the corner, on one side of the large window, she had a beveled, three-paneled mirror over her dressing table and on the other side a large wardrobe with a full length Venetian mirror. Opposite her desk, against the wall, was the famous recamier I slept on during my mother's honeymoon.

One of the stories my mother told me was how this piece of furniture was named after Madame Recamier, a famous French lady, whose portrait was painted by Jacques-Louis David on just such a piece and that in one version she appeared in the nude. When asked if it wasn't uncomfortable, she replied, "No, not at all. The room was very well heated." This story may have been apocryphal, but is nevertheless an illustration of my mother's style. She was of the opinion that fairy tales by the brothers Grimm and Hans Christian Andersen were full of brutality, and too scary for little girls, but that charming vignettes about witty, beautiful ladies, be they naked or otherwise, were perfectly acceptable.

My more pragmatic grandmother, on the other hand, taught me my numbers on her tape measure, quizzed me on my math lessons, helped me to memorize the countless poems I had to recite for school, and introduced me to the mysteries of the sewing machine, among other practicalities.

Grandfather's desk was the focal point of the upstairs library. It was a large, impressive, manly affair with a leather surface and lots of paraphernalia, letters, stationery, and so on. It was absolutely forbidden to touch anything on it. Even the cleaning lady had strict orders to stay away from it. He had increasingly worsening eyesight, which eventually rendered him almost totally blind, so I think it helped him to know where everything was without having to look for it. Next to his desk, on the left side, was a small table with a radio. He listened to a lot of music and very often I listened with him. It was always classical and if they ever sneaked in a lighter piece of some operetta he would grumble. "Pfui," he'd say upon hearing the first few bars of the Merry Widow waltz, which I secretly liked. On the other hand, he really enjoyed operas and he imbued me with a lifetime love affair with them, most of all those written by Mozart. Sometimes he would tell me the storyline of a particular opera, but often we would just listen and I would make up my own stories inspired by the music. In many ways I preferred my versions. The story of Rigoletto was one he did tell me. Rigoletto arranges to have his daughter's seducer killed and, as proof, brought to him in a sack. Things go awry and it is his daughter's body that's delivered to him. During the performance, as I was playing on the carpet, I suddenly looked up and asked, "Is the woman in the bag yet?" Grandfather could hardly contain his amusement and went around telling this story for days, if not years. It became the centerpiece of my bon mot collection.

As years went by, a particular voice, frantic and insistent, was heard with increasing frequency making long speeches in what I knew to be German but didn't understand. My grandfather, and anyone else who happened to be in the room, listened with a solemn expression. The speaker's name was Adolph Hitler.

Noblesse Oblige

Near the end of the school year, my fourth grade class at Gardony Geza elementary school got busy rehearsing for the spring pageant that was to be attended by honored guests, their royal Highnesses, the Archduchess Augusta and Archduke Joseph of Habsburg. Parents and friends were also invited, of course.

The regular teacher, who was even more uptight than usual, and the much maligned music teacher of the school were in charge of the festivities. There was to be a small opera, with music by Zoltan Kodaly, with three principal characters. The girl with the best voice, of course, was chosen, and two boys, one playing her intended and the other his father, a judge. I can still sing every part. The story, briefly, is this: Mari is minding her geese along the banks of the Tisza when the village judge's son comes along and throws something at her geese, thereby indicating his interest in Mari. She goes and complains to his father, who then asks her what she wants for her injured goose. She wants several things, which made absolutely no sense but sounded good, but when she comes to her third request the son cuts in and offers himself, at which point the opera ends with the happy couple holding hands as the rest of the class joins them on stage and sings about true love and more geese.

Before the actual play began, it was customary for a boy and a girl to formally greet the royal couple and for the girl to present her highness with a bouquet. I was the girl honored with this task. This was not a satisfactory situation for the teacher, who chose me only because of my family's social position and who generally could not abide me for reasons known only to her. Nor was it pleasant for me, because I was going through an extremely self-conscious and shy period in my life; one that, for either good or bad, I very shortly overcame. There may have been a connection. The presentation and the speech went off without a hitch, as did the play.

Everyone was to wear "Hungarian dress," which meant navy blue suits with fancy braided buttons for the boys and for the girls little white skirts and blouses with red, white, and green ribbons or rickrack at the hems, a red velvet vest sometimes with embroidery, and a headpiece fashioned much like a tiara, usually also of red velvet with gold or white appliqué.

For my costume, Aunt Valeria chose an authentic and absolutely magnificent native outfit of a mid-calf length skirt elaborately hand embroidered and worn over several cutwork edged petticoats, a crisp white linen blouse, a black velvet bodice, and a headdress of silk embellished with traditional Hungarian wild flowers, wheat stalks, and tiny pearls. I should have been feeling wonderful, but unfortunately I overheard some of the girls whispering, "That isn't a Hungarian dress. Who does she think she is anyway?" I had to admit I didn't look like anyone else there, and due to my delicate condition, I was mortified and crushed.

To make matters worse, the person who came to represent my family was George's older sister, my Aunt Shari, whose husband was a member of Parliament and who herself was the president of an influential women's organization that was founded by my maternal grandmother's sister, the authoress Cecile Tormay. After the play, the pageant moved outdoors for the procession for the viewing pleasure of the honored guests. Two armchairs were placed in the center of the courtyard for the royal couple, but the Archduke graciously offered his seat to my Aunt Shari. Throughout the rest of the ceremony, he stood behind the two ladies with his customary benign expression that he donned for the hundreds of such events he was obliged to attend. As I led the procession, my hand resting on top of Joey's, I knew my goose was cooked in the social circle of the girls of the fourth grade.

The Very Rich were a Little Different

My mother was like a beautiful apparition in my life who took me to special shops in the city or visits to friends in elegant homes, even to her hair salon and the formidable and prestigious bastion where ladies went to have massages and facials, or consulted with the mighty dermatologist who owned the establishment. Once or twice we went to the Hotel Gellert and Spa, a beautiful Arte Nouveau building at the foot of the Gellert Hill on the bank of the Danube, where we took a swim in the crystal clear champagne pool, so named because little spigots of gently bubbling water spurted from the bottom. The water was cool and refreshing and the best when only the two of us were in swimming under the caressing sunlight that shone from the beveled glass ceiling.

I visited many of the villas in our area, but there were two that we went to for tea very often. They were quite different, and both were owned by what I was told very rich people. One was Aunt Mara, who owned a whole city block in Budapest and who came from an old aristocratic family. Her house was elegance itself, somewhat gothic, and full of fascinating and exotic objects such as lampshades with dancing figures or large plumed stuffed birds suspended from the ceiling. Her regal satin mauve and lilac colored bedroom included a beautifully draped antique gold basket where her beloved pug spent his nights. Even the very special dog food was served in gold-edged porcelain dishes made to order by Herend. Aunt Mara also had an all glassed in atrium with exotic tropical plants, bamboo furniture, and divans strewn with brocade cushions. The grounds surrounding her house were similarly landscaped as other gardens in the neighborhood, but in the back she had a large nursery with rows and rows of flowers, and in the center stood a rose-covered gazebo where our summer teas were served on exquisite, almost transparent china. Aunt Mara herself was a formidable woman with very strong opinions, and while she held forth, I would explore the house, sometimes accompanied by one of her many maids in a black dress and a little lace cap and a matching frilly apron.

The other rich lady was rotund, good-natured, and kind. Her husband, Mr. Oroszi, made a lot of money, but was considered nouveau riche and therefore suspect. The house was very grand but somewhat overdone with dark red silk tapestries, a matching set of large overstuffed armchairs, and other oversized and over-the-top furniture As young as I was, I still had a sense that things were a little off, but I enjoyed it as much as Aunt Mara's ancient elegance. My favorite room was the husband's bathroom. The fixtures, including the tub, were shiny black, and the counter with its onyx-looking sink held magnificent tortoise shell brushes and combs, fancy bottles of exotic colognes, and his razor, which was a work of art. On a hook on the back of the door hung his plush black and white striped bathrobe that matched the black and white tiles of the floor. I loved it all. Here again I sometimes explored alone or accompanied by a uniformed maid who later took me to her little room to show me pictures of her family back in the village. The Oroszis were our next-door neighbors and the bottom of their garden against the wild meadows of ours had a large, modern tiled swimming pool and a red clay tennis court. On weekends they always had lots of guests, and often dance music could be heard way into the night

Mr. Oroszi had the good sense to die a year before his country became embroiled in the war, and his wife had to sell the yellow villa and move to an apartment where Mommy and I visited a few times. Her house was bought by the Count and Countess Joseph Szecsenyi, an elderly couple, who moved in with Mademoiselle, who was their children's nanny and French teacher but who continued to live with the old folks. To the horror of Mrs. Oroszi, the brocade wallpaper came down, the walls were painted an off-white, and the house began to look a lot like ours. They even brought in a cow to the converted dressing pavilion near the lovely swimming pool. We got warm, fresh milk every night. Mademoiselle, the loveliest of old ladies, was no Tante Tonchi, and I began to learn French in earnest from her.

Relatives

Of course there were also the relatives. As young women, the mothers of my grandmother and grandfather were friends, so the two families were already close when my grandparents got married. Both had several siblings. My grandfather was one of the seven Szegedy-Maszak offspring, and my grandmother had one sister and two brothers, one of whom was her twin. Most of these siblings eventually acquired wives or husbands and, as a consequence, many children.

Aunt Viola, one of my grandfather's sisters, was widowed early and had no children. She'd come regularly to dine with us, arriving a little after noon and staying even for tea sometimes. She'd help us set the table mostly by walking behind my grandfather and chattering away about family and friends or asking him for medical advice regarding her various ailments. Her hair, like my grandfather's and then my mother's and now mine, never became gray, and she wore it with tight little curls framing her pleasant, round face. She had that square, well-rounded figure that is so characteristic of the Szegedy-Maszak women. Neither my mother nor I escaped this genetic inevitability, and it's there waiting for my still slender daughter and two lovely nieces.

Aunt Viola, wearing Edwardian dresses, usually some shade of purple, with antique lace collars, a brooch at her throat, a watch on a long gold chain, fingers covered with rings, would never come empty-handed.

She had presents for everybody. I usually got fashion magazines, cookies, and always something she crocheted or embroidered.

Uncle Tihamer was also a frequent visitor, and it was his job to keep all the clocks in the house in order. He'd sit at the dining table among parts of our clocks scattered on a blanket in front of him and he cleaned and repaired them while discoursing with my grandfather or was left to himself. He'd stay for tea and then disappear until the clocks began to lose time again.

Aunt Zsuzsi was the youngest of grandfather's three sisters. She married one of his friends he met in medical school who became the family physician, a practice he eventually turned over to their son. I think she was my grandfather's favorite. Tragically, she died quite young of breast cancer. Shortly before her death, in a futile attempt to recover from the then brutal treatments, she came to spend a few weeks at our house away from the city air, and I too became very fond of her. She remembered me in her will and left me a small ruby and diamond ring.

The one truly talented artist of the Barabas grandchildren was Aunt Leone. She was very fond of my mother and used her as a model for several of her paintings. She had no children by either of her husbands and devoted herself to her art and nursing her ailing second husband. By the time I came along, they seldom went anywhere, but I vaguely remember her in a cloud of mauve muslin and wide brimmed hat, drinking tea on the upstairs balcony with my grandparents and mother.

The most solemn and dignified was Aladar senior, my grandfather's oldest brother. He was married to a formidable lady to whom my grandfather always referred to as, "My saint sister-in-law. She's never happy unless she has at least a bishop at her table," he would add. Aunt Charlotte was a big wheel in the Roman Catholic hierarchy and counted even cardinals among her acquaintances.

To me she was all kindness though. Once, toward the end of the war, when I was old enough to go into town by myself, she asked that I come and help with a big citywide fundraising effort. It was a big event. Beautiful young actresses with their little collection baskets were photographed for the newspapers. My territory was near the famous Chain Bridge. Afterwards, she invited me to dine in her severely elegant apartment, but alas no bishops came. Only her husband and her son joined us at the table. Both father and son were named Aladar. In the family, the son was known as Aladar Junior and even when he and my mother were in their eighties, that's how she referred to him. The younger Aladar was in the diplomatic service and had played a major role in Hungary's efforts to extricate itself from the Fascist yoke. It was he who was sent by the Regent to negotiate a separate peace with the Allies toward the end of the war. This effort eventually landed him in the concentration camp of Mauthausen. During the short freedom that Hungary enjoyed after the war and before the Iron Curtain descended upon it, he was sent to Washington as the Hungarian Ambassador. When the Communists took over, Aladar asked for and was granted political asylum and spent the rest of his life in the United States working as editor for the *Voice of America*. He became a very special friend with Mommy and George and was best man at my first wedding.

Father as a young officer in the Hungarian Cavalry.

Father at tea in the downstairs library of the Old House.

Mommy in mourning holding baby Vivi.

Grandfather, Grandmother, and Nanny doting on me.

The Winter of 1940 at Lake Balaton. I am in
my stunning Norwegian ensemble.

Grandfather and I with our Puli dog on a garden path.

The last photo taken of me in Hungary by Zdenko just before he left for the Soviet front.

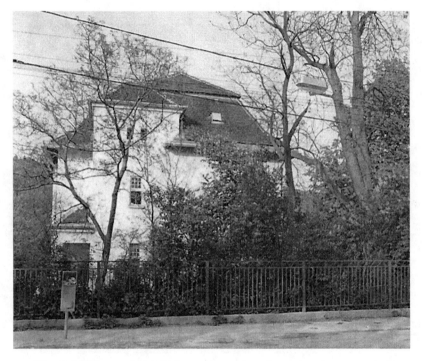

The Old House (1984) from the side - the second story window of the bathroom I locked myself in before we left in 1944.

George, Uncle Andrew and Uncle Julius-ready for a ride. Circa 1939.

The brothers' reunion in Toronto, Canada, in 1989.

The War is Nearing

I don't remember exactly when the bombings started. After years of careful and intense diplomacy and desperate political maneuverings to avoid entering the war, in 1941 the Hungarian government was forced to join the Axis powers, primarily because of the enormous threat the Soviet Union posed for the country.

For the first few years of the war, life in the old house went on more or less as it did before. The news was bad and there were some shortages. The young men who came to work in our garden, the boy who brought our dinners, and our very own gardener, Veti's father, were all called up for the army. My uncle, for some reason, was exempt, perhaps because of his age or because a much-wanted child was born to him and Aunt Valeria after several miscarriages. Told he was a beautiful baby, I was surprised to see the ugly little wrinkled thing, but soon he became an interesting phenomenon to observe. I didn't feel that my ten year reign as princess had come to an end at all. As it turned out it had, but not only because of the arrival of my cousin Mihaly.

In the fall of 1943, I started prep school at the Baar-Madas Gymnasium as a half-boarder, meaning I attended classes in the morning in the school wing, then walked over to the other wing of the building for my noon meal and for the rest of the day. A variety of private lessons were available to students. I took piano and French. We were required also to have an organized daily constitutional, which I took with my French class, walking in rows of two and speaking only French. This type of school for young ladies was called gymnasium and had four years of lower and four of upper classes. At the end of eight years, at graduation, students had an equivalent of an American Associate of Arts degree. The first year we were all very proud to wear our new uniforms and caps with the school emblem. Upperclassmen were sick and tired of it and could hardly wait to put on their modish frocks and high heels as soon as school was out for weekends or vacations.

Some time each afternoon was devoted to socializing in large, comfortable dayrooms, where we could just talk or play ping-pong or board games. Other times we were invited to "tea parties" by upperclassmen in their quarters upstairs, where we were obliged to play games and perform on the piano or recite some poem as part of winning or losing at the games. In the beginning, I was very much intimidated by being surrounded with all those glamorous and accomplished young ladies, and found such gatherings almost unbearable.

I was much more comfortable with outdoor recreations, particularly the tennis courts, and especially when they were turned into ice rinks during the winter. Activities ended with afternoon tea in the dining room, after which we adjourned to our study room to do our homework under the supervision of a deaconess. We each had a designated study partner, and I was fortunate to have been paired with Daisy, the only other girl in the school with an English name, who very soon became my special friend. In the evening, I was picked up by my mother or another adult and we made our way down the hillside a few blocks to the main road, where we caught the Number 83 streetcar to our home.

One evening Mommy came with George in his car. He had just returned from a business trip to Berlin, and brought back a large can of black market American coffee, a new, state-of-the-art record player with plenty of Kurt Furtwangler recordings, and the certainty that Germany had lost the war. He was cautioned to hold his tongue, a quality that didn't come easy for him. I heard no more. Grown-ups were very careful what they spoke about in front of the children lest they let something slip that could land everyone in serious peril.

The German invasion came in March of 1944, exactly a month before my eleventh birthday on April 19. Soldiers could be seen everywhere.

A Wehrmacht panzer division was quartered in our neighborhood. I'd watch from the upstairs sitting room window as the troops did their morning calisthenics on the meadow of the ski jump. One day a tank got stuck in the irrigation ditch on the side of the meadow to the great delight of a few bystanders. Some snickerings were heard in Hungarian about the mighty German machinery.

Homeowners in the neighborhood were required to provide lodgings for the soldiers. In our house, the downstairs library was assigned to two towheaded boys, one barely sixteen. They were shy, soft-spoken, and probably homesick and frightened. Veti and I played ball with them and practiced our linguistic and budding flirting skills. On Easter, my grandmother sent down to them some ham, colored eggs, and a loaf of our special braided Easter bread. It had been a long time since they'd had such abundance, and they were visibly moved. More than likely it was the one good meal they had before being sent off to their certain deaths in some frozen battlefield of the eastern front.

The bombs kept on falling. The sound of the warning sirens became routine. Night after night, I'd get ready for bed only to be roused before I had a chance to fall asleep to go down to the hallway in the basement that was fixed up with cots and armchairs. I had to dress just in case we had to get out, but I just crawled half asleep into one of the cots and usually slept through the attacks. We were fortunate in that most of the bombs were dropped on the Pest side over the industrial part of town, and the only time our neighborhood was hit was by an errant shell from one of the large anti-aircraft guns stationed on top of the hills behind our house. It hit directly on the mental institution just a block from our house, and the next day a group of bewildered patients came down to the streetcar stop on our corner with two nurses to take them to some safer place, wherever that may have been. Grandmother and George usually went up to the roof during the raids to watch the terrible yet beautiful fireworks and to report to us. Sometimes they would hurriedly rush in and we knew it was getting closer. My grandmother never lost her calm. She was a woman always in command of herself. One time when she'd gone up to get something important from the dining room that she forgot, a small incendiary bomb flew in the open window. She calmly picked it up and threw it back out.

We learned to distinguish the sound of airplanes and the direction from which they came. If they came from the east we were in for an easier time, but the unmistakable drone of a B-24 formation from the west meant serious business. Nevertheless, I don't recall ever being very frightened, partly because I always felt safe in the old house with my grandparents, but perhaps also because as a child, for good or for bad, I had a way of accepting things as they were. Yet, now and then, perhaps triggered by a low flying plane overhead, I still hear the droning of heavy bombers and the incessant barrage of explosion upon explosion inter-twined like drawings of circles, and I can actually feel clutching my soft blue pillow. It is true that I wasn't frightened. It was beyond that. It was surreal. I suppose what I describe is the birth of classic post-traumatic syndrome, call it disorder if you like, and its accompanying denial.

The Summer of 1944

On a balmy June day, my grandmother, mother, and I went shop-ping on a sunlit street lined with fashionable boutiques up in the Castle District of Buda. The three of us strolled leisurely from shop to shop, inspecting the various displays of the latest fashions. Flowery prints were all the rage. Beautiful young ladies teetering on the new style of high-wedged sandals strolled the avenue in flowery skirts and dresses that swung in the early summer breeze. My mother and I wore identical skirts with a pattern of colorful tulips, hers with black background and mine with blue. We were all in a good mood. I was happy and comfortable with a sense of accomplishment. I had just successfully completed my first year of higher education and had nothing but a summer of fun to look forward to. We bought a red belt for a new blue and white striped cotton dress our seamstress was making for me along with two others, all for the first time sewn with darts on the bodice. I was growing up and filling out in just the right places. My new bathing suit, a beautiful lime green with some sort of green pattern, was cut with small cups. My mother bought it hurriedly after she saw me, fortunately in the privacy of our own swimming pool, in last year's suit and concluded that I needed more cover-up than a year ago.

One of my new dresses was made of an exquisite taffeta fabric from a suit originally made for my grandmother's trousseau. I was to wear it at the unveiling of my grandmother's now deceased sister's bust in one of the squares of Budapest. Cecile Tormay was a well-known and much re-spected author and women's rights activist, the founder of an important political and social women's organization. Some of her books were made into films. She was and still is considered an important writer. One of her novels, somewhat modeled on our family history, is called *Old House*. She died when I was still very little and I barely remember her.

This was, of course, a momentous occasion for the Tormay family, and we prepared for it with due reverence. My grandmother and her two brothers were to be part of the ceremony, with their families, my aunts and uncles, and several cousins in attendance. Every one of us was beau-tifully and appropriately dressed for the occasion. Not only did I have a new elegant dress, but my mother took me to her hairdresser, who un-furled my long thick braids and with her professional expertise, created an array of soft curls that cascaded down my back.

A surprising number of people gathered in the little square. At the appropriate time, a black limousine arrived; the Regent, Miklos Horthy, emerged, accompanied by his wife and his incredibly beautiful daughter-in-law with her small son. Both ladies had sheer black veils and were in deep mourning because the Regent's son had recently died in the wreckage of his fighter plane. The official word was that he died a hero's death for his country, but rumor had it that in the midst of a drunken party on the airfield, he decided to do some aerial acrobatics that caused the crash.

The Regent came and the unveiling took place; he placed flowers at the base of the sculpture, made a speech, shook the hands of the two male siblings of the honoree, and kissed my grandmother's hand. They each stepped back. After some cordial exchanges among the ladies, a few official photographs taken, the Horthys returned to their limousine and drove away. Our family was in a festive mood. In the one unofficial picture I have left, it is obvious that people were caught unawares and the smiles are charmingly genuine. It is a true snapshot. The festivities ended, as usual for those times, with the early warning sirens of an air raid. We dispersed. It was the last time my mother and I saw any of them. Nor did I ever put on my taffeta dress again. We left it, less then a year later, on the side of an icy highway in the Austrian Alps as we fled from the fast approaching marauding hordes from the east.

But that was later. The magical summer of 1944 still lay ahead of me.

The Village Called Vezseny

Mommy and George were looking for a vacation home for us. We began to spend part of our summers at his aunt's house in a small fishing village on the bank of the River Tisza at the edge of the great plains. This beautiful great river, the second largest in Hungary, a country of many rivers, runs east of and parallel to the Danube. As it flows from the east it bends toward the south, somewhat mirroring the path of the Danube and eventually, near the Yugoslav border, flows into the Danube; after that, the river makes its eastward turn homeward to the Black Sea.

The village was a relatively short drive from Budapest; we just had to cross the region between the two rivers almost in a straight line. Usually George drove us in his beloved Adler convertible, but sometimes my mother and I would take the train to a larger town nearby, where we were picked up by a landau (a fancy horse and buggy operation) from the rectory. On my favorite trip, we took a ship from the large town and climbed down a rope ladder to a waiting rowboat at our destination. The man who picked us up from the ship was the same trusty, sun-browned, chiseled-faced fisherman who took us all across the river each morning and afternoon to the sandy beaches on the opposite shore.

George's aunt was the widow of the circuit judge of the region, but they maintained a rather simple house, much like any other house of the villagers, with a few added modern conveniences, such as an indoor toilet and an extra room that served as office and library for the judge. The gentry of the village seemed all to be related to one another in some way or other. The postmistress who operated her duties from her home was the mother of the Presbyterian minister, whose sister was married to an artist and who lived in the only proper villa and owned the only automobile in the town.

The minister was a portly, cheerful, and gregarious gentleman with a zest for living. His wife was a wiry little woman who performed the duties of her station in life with energy and enthusiasm. They had two sons, one a year younger than I and the other a few years older. The parsonage, which was the hub of all social activities, was a rambling, substantial, one-story stone building with a spacious and comfortable veranda that served as living and dining room during the summer. After Sunday services, the elders of the parish would gather there in their sober black suits to ceremoniously finish the Communion wine and the bread. The important formalities over, the rest of the day was given to gaiety, good food and wine, and talking and laughter way into the night. We older children would hang out and did our own share of gossiping and laughing and playing under the large, sheltering trees, while the harvest moon played tricks with the lighting of the balmy summer night. Sometimes I would get tired before my parents were ready to go and half lying on the wooden bench in the large, grapevine-covered arbor, I'd dreamily listen to the music, often Caruso records, that emanated from the house, until the party was over and we'd make the short walk to our house by the river, where I'd be asleep before my head hit the pillow.

For a pampered Budapest girl, one who has only been to fashionable watering places and winter resorts, village life was an exotic and marvelously different experience, albeit not without its occasional pitfalls. To this day, I don't know how I "mistreated" a girl I was trying to make friends with, but an old woman followed me on the other side of the street all the way from my aunt's house to the post office, cursing me and telling me what a spoiled rotten girl I was with my uppity city ways and that I should be ashamed of myself for treating a sweet innocent girl the way I did. I think even my aunt thought of me as spoiled and a bit arrogant—not without some merit, I must confess. At home, I was never asked to make my bed or to clear the table, and thus it never occurred to me that I was expected to do so. Knowing the lyrics to some Mozart aria in perfect Italian or having read all of Mark Twain didn't cut it with her; however, I did eventually make up with the offended girl and I gave her one of my dresses she admired.

I never stopped being scared by the hissing gaggles of geese that grazed along the riverbank because they were truly dangerous. But I could walk calmly along the sidewalks when the cows came home each evening from the fields. Then, to top it all, one morning I was awakened by crescendos of incredible shrieking that went on ceaselessly for all the better part of the morning. I was informed by the housemaid, who obviously enjoyed my incredulous reaction, that this was the day the vet came to town to castrate all the young male pigs in the village and not anything to get all bent out of shape about.

Of course, I also experienced some lovely, pleasurable times, like cutting clusters of sun-warmed grapes from the small vineyard in the back of our house for our dinner table, walking along the undulating ocean of the famous golden wheat fields and picking red poppies and blue cornflowers that grew along the side of the path, and once, during a sunset walk toward the end of my last summer there, having my arm tremble, ever so slightly, as it brushed against a young man's arm.

But the best, the most important, the great love of my life, was the river itself. The banks of the Tisza along the village were lined with reed-filled bogs where the geese could tug at tufts of watery grasses, and small rambling willows, not tall enough to block the view, grew all the way up to the road. It was lovely to look at but not much good for anything else. The other side, however, was blessed by long sandy beaches. Each morning, shortly after breakfast, we'd walk over to where the big rowboats of the fishermen were moored and were taken to the other side. After the noon meal and a short nap, most of us returned for another roundtrip to the beach.

I spent much of my time by myself, learning to be more and more at home in the water, catching its rhythm, allowing it to carry me, to become one with the gentle rolling of the waves, or experimenting with different strokes to swim against the current. Other times I would walk far upstream on the warm sand, enjoying the feel of its texture under my feet, until the heat sent me back among the beckoning cool waves to half float and half swim back where the others were.

Of course, there were lots of different sizes of boats, and eventually I became a very good oarsman. I especially loved working with skulls if an owner was kind enough to let me borrow one. I usually had to prove my competence before that happened, and I am proud to say nobody ever refused me.

The summer of 1944, when I was eleven years old, I was sent down for the entire month of August, primarily to get me out of the city where the bombing raids were unrelenting. In retrospect, the responsibility of having me there without my parents in such times was extremely difficult for my aunt and, with the exception of my solitary times with the river, it was also stressful for me. Navigating in the treacherous rural social world in the last few months of my prepubescence proved to be more daunting than the deep, fast flowing, large river that was the Tisza.

There were other more serious concerns as well. The Russian army had broken through the eastern border of Hungary by now. Rumors and facts about the war intermingled. My aunt heard that the river was being poisoned by the enemy and would not let me go swimming for a few days. As soon as we found out this was not true, I stopped pouting and got back into the water.

In so many ways, this last summer in Vezseny was magical, and yet the very air was permeated with an ominous sense of imminent disaster. It was a great relief when my mother arrived to take me back home to Budapest.

The Return to Budapest

This time there was no comfortable carriage to carry us to the train station. A farmer took us in a wagon drawn by a mare whose foal, tied loosely by a rope to the back, dutifully followed. My mother sat with the driver, and I sat in back with my bronzed summer legs dangling over the dusty roads as we passed first between the white-washed cottages with their window boxes of red geraniums, then through the gypsy section at the edge of the village where their little brown kids in their short cotton shirts and bare bottoms stopped their play to stare at us. I'd wave at some of them and they waved back, some even running a little ways behind or next to the wagon. Once the village disappeared in a cloud of dust from my view, we continued on to the train station between the great wheat fields, now silent and resting until it was time for the earth to be turned again and replanted for next year's harvest. When we first arrived for our vacation during the time of wheat harvest, these fields bustled with harvesters among the golden stalks of grain and shirtless young men on top of combines, their bodies glistening in the hot sun. Past the wheat fields, a row of cottonwoods, their leaves shimmering in the now waning summer sun, lined the road that now rejoined the path of the river for the last leg of our trek to our destination.

The train station was full of people. It was the first of my many experiences with wartime train travel. People were coming and going who knows where all over Europe in those days. Soldiers, some coming off leave going back to their units, some going home with bandaged wounds or leaning on crutches, peasants with bundles, mothers with screaming children, all trying to get on the already crowded coaches. There was standing room only. We were packed in so no one could stand without being pushed and tugged by bodies from all sides. A soldier took pity on me and invited me to stand on his rugged combat boots. He said he would not even feel the weight of such a slip of a girl. I took his suggestion, which under the circumstances didn't seem strange at all, and gently put my sandals over his feet. He assured me it was fine. The train lurched forward and began its journey. Sometimes my face brushed against the roughness of the soldier's tunic—there was no way to avoid our bodies from touching but there was nothing sensual about it. It was the first of countless wartime incidents when an unexpected and sudden kindness was offered to me. A chance meeting, a fleeting moment of instant intimacy and kinship that can never happen in normal times. And so we traveled in silence while the train picked up speed and roared its way toward the west

There were some exclamations of surprise and even some shrieks of horror as we entered Budapest through its industrial eastern suburbs and saw, many of us for the first time, the horrific devastation the air raids had caused. We pulled into Eastern Railway Station. Unbeknownst to us, in a few weeks, caravans of boxcars carrying our friends, our schoolmates, our neighbors, would depart from here to places no one has ever heard of: Dachau, Mauthausen, Auschwitz-Birkenau.

I have no clear recollection of the sequence of events after our return to the old house from summer vacation, nor do I wish to attempt to arrange it in any particular order. I feel the fact that it is all jumbled up in my mind fits the times perfectly. I certainly was happy to be with my grandparents again. Throughout my early childhood, it was my mother who took me places, who bought things for me, who chose the schools and activities, but it was with my grandparents that I spent most of my everyday life. Consequently, I was very close to them and I trusted them explicitly.

Those few months in the fall of 1944 unfold as a montage of visual memories. Snapshots of scenes really more than events. There is one, in the filtered sunlight of early September, of my little cousin, Mihaly, now fourteen months old, sitting on a blanket on the lawn wearing a little visor cap and a striped sweater vest my mother knitted for him.

Another of Zdenko, my half-brother, handsome in his soldier's uniform as he and I stroll in the garden. He brings the developed picture of my favorite photo of me that day, and he stays for tea, as always, before we say our good-byes. He is going to the eastern front, which by now is not very far away.

School begins, but only regular morning classes, and we spend even those times mostly in the basement watched by a deaconess while we listen to the now all too familiar droning of airplanes followed by barrages of explosions and occasionally, a long, scary whistle. But it's seldom as close as in my neighborhood at home. Some girls make fun of my shoes because of their small platform soles. They think I am trying to be all grown up and it hurts my feelings, mainly because they are right. We may now wear whatever shoes we can get for our always growing feet, but we are still in uniforms. A lot of girls from last year did not come back to school. Some felt safer in their homes in the countryside and some had left Hungary altogether. My special friend and study partner, Daisy, who is Jewish, is mercifully already in Switzerland with her parents.

There are other shortages besides leather shoes. We still have food. After all, Hungary is "the breadbasket of Europe." Fuel is the big problem. Aunt Valeria's fourteen-year-old nephew and I gather horse chestnuts in our garden and haul them in gunnysacks or baskets to wherever they can be used as substitute for coal. We ride the streetcars and have a little flirtation going on between us.

German soldiers everywhere. A few people we meet on the streets have a yellow star sewn on their coats. A woman in tattered clothes, eyes crazed with bewilderment, comes to our gate. She's lost everything and everyone in an air raid. Fall is here. The world turns black and white and very gray.

I have read a great deal about what happened in Hungary during 1944 and although there are many different accounts, all of them agree on the following: On March 19, 1944, the German army occupied the country ostensibly by "invitation." The Regent Miklos Horthy's government did everything in its power to save the nation and all its people from the fate that befell other German occupied countries. In the beginning, these efforts met with some measurable success.

In August, secret negotiations with the Allies took place. Hungary would surrender and lay down its arms. But because the country was by now full of German soldiers, and its own Nazi party, the Arrow Cross, was gaining power, the surrender had to remain secret. The Soviets, however, true to form, leaked the information to the Germans and on October 15, 1944, the government was taken over by the Arrow Cross party in a coup, primarily engineered by the Germans, and a reign of terror followed. People were arrested, many were executed, most were tortured, and quite a number of them, including my Uncle Aladar, shipped off to concentration camps as political prisoners.

I am not writing history. I am writing my story, but these events had a direct impact on my life and by then I was aware of what was going on. My last day at school was either the day before or the day of the coup. After that, we didn't leave our houses for several days. George's car had been "requisitioned for the war effort" some time ago and the streetcars ran intermittently. In any case, it was dangerous to walk on the streets, even in our own neighborhood. We were in the weird position where we could have just as likely been bombed by the Axis as by the Allies.

A Decision Had to be Made

That fateful autumn day in 1944, I locked myself into the upstairs bathroom. The adults stood outside the door while my mother cajoled and begged me, and others took turns trying to convince me or reason with me to please unlock the door. I would not. I could not. I stood in the middle of the large bathroom with the key in my hand, contemplating throwing it out the window. In the end, my resolve worn down, I capitulated and it was I who turned the key to the bathroom door.

While all this drama was going on, a large, black sedan was waiting, fully packed, in the backyard by the double gate. Not the sleek little Adler, but someone else's automobile whose owner, now chaufferless, didn't know how to drive. The owner wanted it taken to Sopron, a town near the Austrian border in the far western region of Hungary, and it was the place George and my mother decided to go to join some of George's family. We were going there, temporarily, until things settled down. It was best to get out of town. Only a few kilometers to the east, the Russians were pillaging and raping their way toward the liberation of Budapest.

The rest of that day blends into the November fog. I found out later that I was given a mild sedative, but I do remember standing in the yard saying almost perfunctory farewells to a small gathering of household members. My grandmother and my best friend Veti stood side by side. I don't know if my grandfather was there, but then again I think he must have been. The gardener's wife was going grocery shopping and George said she might as well come with us, as we were going by the market. I always thought it was ironic that the last person to whom I said goodbye that day was someone I barely knew.

George started the engine and drove out the gate. We went along the streetcar track to the next block, turned right and, after we dropped off our passenger, we careened onto the main highway lined with the now leafless chestnut trees, past my elementary school, past my Great Aunt Emma's villa with the stone lions at the gate, amidst silent woods, out of the city and toward the west.

December 25th was less than a month away. I was eleven years and eight months old, and as we made our way through the countryside away from everything I had ever known, I knew in the depth of my soul that I would never walk with my grandfather to the pharmacy we just passed, or rake the golden leaves of autumn with my grandmother, that Veti and I would grow up without each other, and that I would never spend another Christmas here or see any of the people whom we left standing in the foggy garden of the old house. And so it was.

Sopron

Shortly after we left Budapest, the sedative took effect and I fell asleep for almost the entire trip. It was almost nightfall when we arrived in the beautiful Baroque city of Sopron in the northwest region of Hungary near the Austrian border and, according to a brochure, "only a short train ride" from Vienna. Of course, if one didn't have the proper papers, Vienna might as well have been on the moon in the turmoil of the near end of the war, and especially during the Cold War that followed. We actually did have passports, but we stayed in the town, not knowing exactly what our next move would be.

In the interim, we settled in town with George's brother, Uncle Andrew, his wife Aunt Magda, and my step-cousin Madge who had left Budapest some time earlier. We shared the former corner salon of an elegant Baroque home that now served as a pensione a sort of boarding house mostly for refugees such as we. Madge, a year older than I, was a big boned, tall girl, with a tiny turned up nose that gave the illusion of pulling her upper lip with it.

One corner of the room had large curved windows overlooking a plaza. Two more windows on either side were facing the two avenues that led to the plaza, so sitting at the side window we were looking at an equally lovely Baroque building across the way. It was definitely a cityscape. The only things remaining from the former grandeur of the salon were a beautiful baby grand Bosendorfer piano, now pushed to one corner, and a magnificent crystal chandelier in the middle of the room. Because of a shortage of beds, some guests were provided with cots. Madge and I shared a rather narrow one. We slept head to foot; she complained more than I, albeit cheerfully, although, because of her height, her feet were frequently in my way. After a while, the most interesting and delightful member of the family joined us sporting a pompadour and wearing a checkered sport coat to the chagrin of his father. It was Andrew Junior. He was seventeen or eighteen by then and his only ambitions, in addition to annoying his father, were to play American jazz on the piano and chase girls, both of which he did with considerable skill and enthusiasm. Some nights he'd sit in the lotus position at the end of Madge's and my cot next to the piano, wearing his maroon and gray striped pajamas, and bang out some wonderful pieces. In no time at all I learned the words, in Hungarian of course, to such classics as *My Heart Belongs to Daddy*, which I know to this day.

All of the rooms were occupied. Some people stayed longer, some for only a few days. A noon meal was served to everyone in the large dining room. The owner of the establishment, a widow, appeared only at these occasions, and her apartments at one end of the house were never opened to any of the lodgers. I don't know if she was a Nazi sympathizer or used her connection to protect her guests, but she did have several SS officers among her acquaintances. One time, she announced to everyone that she had invited a few high ranking German officers for a private supper in her quarters. Madge and I were told to be absolutely quiet and stay out of sight. Nevertheless, we managed to sneak a furtive peek at the formidable guests as they arrived in the impressive uniforms of the infamous elite Schutzstaffel (SS). For whatever reason, we could barely stifle our involuntary giggling. Our mothers were furious and we managed to content ourselves with covering our mouths and sharing our mirth only with our eyes. I suppose it was our way of dealing with the palpable and almost unbearable anxiety that permeated the house.

People kept arriving and leaving. One family with two little girls stayed only long enough to infect some of the children, me included, with head lice. My mother took me to a doctor who recommended washing my hair with turpentine. It worked, but it was a horrible experience. After the initial treatment, it took what seemed like hours each day while my mother, whistling unconsciously under her breath, combed my long tresses almost hair by hair until we could be certain that I was free of lice eggs. It nearly drove me crazy. I had hoped for some time for a more grown-up hairdo than my long pigtails, and this experience convinced my mother. She took me to a hairdresser for a cut and perm. I had envisioned something quite glamorous, but alas, I just looked like a little girl with shorter and kinkier hair. To add insult to injury, the hairdresser even put two little bows on either side of my face. I was in tears as we walked home and was even more embarrassed when everyone elaborately complimented my new look.

Soon I forgot all about it because while my mother and I had the community bathroom to ourselves one afternoon, I suffered a terrible burn on the back of my upper arm from a hot pipe over the tub. We had to go back to the doctor for several treatments with some sort of salve and fresh bandages. It took a long time to heal and didn't get any better until one day when the bandage stuck to it my mother gently poured warm water over it to loosen the gauze. After that, it healed in a matter of a few days, but I carried the scar for many years.

I wasn't the only one to give my mother cause for alarm. George could also be a handful. One afternoon, the two of them returned from an errand in an obviously agitated state. At one point that afternoon, George spotted his confiscated Adler convertible parked alongside a curb. He recognized it because during an air raid in Budapest the top was cut by falling glass and he had repaired it with tape. A young woman was sitting in the passenger seat, so George walked up to her and asked what she was doing in his car. She informed him that the car belonged to SS Major So and So, who was expected any moment. Fortunately, my mother was able to pull the indignant and very angry George away without any further confrontation and before the officer arrived.

The war was ever present in daily life but, nevertheless, the young people who lived in the pensione, especially the teenagers, found all types of activities to while away the schoolless, waiting game days with socializing, parlor games, and occasional rough-housings. After the dishes from the noon meal were cleared away, the dining room became a favorite hangout. Now and then, the older teenagers were entrusted to take the gang to an afternoon movie. A preponderance of German propaganda films dominated the playbills. These were beautifully made, always with an extremely handsome Aryan hero, often a member of the Hitler Youth Corps, doing brave deeds for the glory of the Third Reich. I particularly remember the Nazi version of the Titanic saga in which a young German ship officer, again quite drop-dead gorgeous, tries to talk the stupid English captain and crew out of running their ship into the iceberg. But would they listen? We also saw a lot of Zarah Leander movies. She was the replacement for the renegade deserter, Marlene Dietrich, but her films were more in the Joan Crawford style and I found them a bit beyond me and quite boring. Zarah was also a chanteuse whose dark, throaty voice was frequently heard on the radio. We also saw Hungarian movies, and were quite excited when one of our best-loved comediennes, Vasari Piri, came to our boarding house and had lunch with us one day. She was merely one of several people who stopped only overnight on their way to the west.

Our boarding house was especially desirable because the proprietress had built a small cone-shaped bunker of reinforced concrete. This weird mound took up almost all of the small courtyard in the back of the house, and even though it was grass covered, it pretty much disfigured what at one time must have been a lovely garden. But in the end, it did save many lives, very likely mine included.

We had little if any reliable news of how the war was going. Radio broadcasts or newspapers were mostly propaganda. The best source of information was usually the newly arrived guests. Some who had been in besieged towns that were taken by the enemy and then taken back were adamant about not falling into Russian hands again.

A small room next to ours was for a time occupied by the Countesses Szecsenyi, distant relations of our Budapest neighbors. The three daughters of the long divorced Count Balint Szecsenyi and a Russian princess were Alexandra, nineteen, with black hair, Francesca, seventeen, with red hair, and Beatrix, not yet sixteen, who was movie star beautiful with long, smooth, platinum blonde hair. Balint, who only came once for a short afternoon visit dressed in traditional Austrian hunting costume, was a stocky block of a man with a fierce black mustache.

I admired Beatrix, and both Madge and I became her friend. One afternoon, she asked us to accompany her on a visit to her mother's apartment in the inner city. The Princess welcomed us in a flowery silk robe that frequently fell open, revealing a shiny, beige nightgown with lace appliqué. She was tall and angular, yet seemed soft like a pillow, a little out of focus, her silhouette a bit smudged, and spoke with a heavy Russian accent, languidly and haltingly as though she might fall asleep any moment. She was fastidiously attended by her companion, a charming, effete man of an uncertain age and indefinable nationality. To me, she was the quintessential aristocratic Russian émigré. Madge was slightly disgusted however. But then Madge probably hadn't waded her way through the novel, *War and Peace,* as I did the previous summer. "She was very Tolstoy," I reported about the princess to my mother, who laughed, which was good to hear. Mommy didn't laugh a lot in those days. The Szecsenyi girls moved on shortly thereafter, just before the air raids began.

In the early part of our stay, Sopron was for some reason not bombed. We had almost daily air raid warnings, but the planes flew over us again and again. After a while, the people relaxed and frequently did not heed the sirens. It was for this reason that in many towns the first attack was the most deadly.

That is exactly what happened on St. Nicholas day, December 6, 1944. Santa Claus comes to European children earlier than in the States. That's the day the shoes are put out and if one was good, one got nice sweets and interesting little toys, but if not, the gifts were pieces of coal or onions. Well, I guess we were not very good that year because what we got was a rain of huge bombs. Doors flew open, parents grabbed their children, briefcases were snatched up, and there was general confusion and a lot of shouting as we all ran, scrunched over, as though that would help get us to the bunker and down the steps as fast as we could. The Budapest bombings I had experienced were child's play compared to what came down from the skies over us for the next several weeks each and every day and night.

Some of the older boys were hiking in the nearby woods that first day. The usual plan was to cross the railroad tracks and be out of harm's way in case of a real raid, but unfortunately the planes entirely missed the tracks and instead cut a swath through the southern end of the epic Vienna woods. Our boys got on their stomachs and were thrown about by the undulating earth for quite sometime, but they all made it back safely. Not all hikers were that lucky.

We were always told that all windows should be open during raids. The only window left with glass after the first raid was the one I forgot to open. The chandelier survived for a while, but during a later attack it was pulverized and lay on the parquet like a mound of fine snow. One apartment building was sheared in half, and, as we were navigating among the ruins, we could see half-rooms, some with pictures on the wall and furniture still intact. Some of the kids came home triumphantly one day with piles of cellophane-wrapped candies that scattered in the debris after the sweet shop took a direct hit.

After a while, we could pretty well figure the approximate time between air raids so that we could run an errand or catch an early movie. One evening we managed to see an entire play at a somewhat damaged but still imposing Baroque theatre with yet another fleeing stage star. And perhaps most memorable of all, on another evening, before the chandelier got destroyed, my parents invited all the people in the pensione to a chamber concert by good friends from the Budapest Music Academy. For a short while, the house was filled with beautiful and poignant music, so soothing to ears accustomed lately only to explosions, the terrifying whistling of weaponry, crashing debris, and the shattering of glass.

In time, we learned the code of the Austrian radio station and knew without waiting for the warning siren when to prepare for another attack. The code word for our area was "spinat, spinat," which is German for "spinach," and for the rest of our lives together Mommy and I used it to give each other warning: "Spinat, spinat," we'd say and we'd smile at each other because, after all, we lived to tell the tale.

On Christmas Eve, 1944, we called my grandparents in Budapest. As we spoke to my grandmother on the phone, she told us that through the falling snow she could see the outline of soldiers with rifles pointed, silently and carefully walking along the streetcar tracks. The Soviet army had circled the city and first entered from the west. By the next day, all telephone lines to the capital were dead. The Soviets laid siege to Budapest for seven weeks before it fell, on February 13, 1945.

Exactly three months after that first raid on December 6, 1944 and only days after Mommy, George, and I had fled the country, the city of Sopron, reduced to a pile of Baroque rubble and almost completely destroyed, was captured by the Soviet army on March 6, 1945. It was one of the last Hungarian towns to fall, and in less than a month, the whole of Hungary was under Soviet control.

The world, as I had known it, had come to an end. The spoils now belonged to the marauding hordes from the east and a new dark age descended on the land that gave me life.

The Flight from Hungary

There were seventeen of us who stole away in a bus with a trailer from Sopron on a freezing evening in the early spring of 1945. Our departure time was delayed because of a horrendous air raid upon the city right after the noon meal. In fact, between the air raid and the time to board the bus, I didn't have time enough to put on the outfit my mother and I picked for the trip, and was still dressed in my little pleated navy blue serge school uniform. It was to be the mainstay of my entire wardrobe for the next several years. I like to say I set the precedent for the miniskirt. The trailer held most of our luggage and the people in the bus only carried absolute necessities and the all important "papers." In addition, my mother was carrying a chamois pouch, filled with jewelry, tied to her waist. There were pins and rings with diamonds, rubies, emeralds, and pearls, gold bracelets, and the dangling diamond earrings that once deco-rated my bandages during my middle ear infection days six years before. In the subsequent years, one by one, these jewels were sold for food and lodging.

On the bus, I found a place on some boxes near the rear door with my head resting between my arms on a large brown suitcase. I tried but could not sleep and for a long time I entertained myself by spinning a long story of what heroic role I'd play in helping the fight for victory. Sometime dur-ing my reverie, we crossed the border and entered Austria.

Our plan, though not specific, was to get as far west as possible into the British, French, or most especially the American Zones. These lines were pre-designated places by the Allies and sometimes the Americans had to sit and wait for the Russians to come to claim their territory. By now, most of the Axis effort of the fighting was to thwart the advance of the Russian army.

Sometime the next day we came to a hill too steep for our vehicle's big load. It was decided to unhook the trailer and, while the bus took the people up the mountain, a few men, George among them, would watch the luggage until the empty bus came back for it. When the bus returned, the Soviet troops were visible to the naked eye and the men decided not to bother with the complicated hook up and to get the hell out of there. They grabbed a few pieces of the luggage, but had to abandon most of the bigger pieces. We were just glad to see the men safe. In a day or so, after we passed a few closed gas stations, the fuel ran out and we all had to get out of the bus to continue on foot. We could only carry what was absolutely necessary and nothing very heavy. This was the only time I saw George cry. He was holding one of his treasured books as he sat on the side of the road in a momentary abject despair. It made me afraid.

All of us, at one time or another, hit that moment of realization that this surreal world was in fact our only reality. Yet, strange as it may sound, throughout my life there were moments when I felt that those were the times when I was truly free. No rules, no possessions, no responsibilities, no future, a past lost. Only the Now existed. I've heard others express similar feelings, and I believe that this may very well be a component of the aftermath of whatever combat veterans experience. "Yeah, it was bad, but I was alive and it was better than this boring—(fill in the blank)."

We continued on foot with our scant belongings, not knowing how or when we would eat again, or where we were going to sleep that night. We were not alone. We met many people on the road, saw lots of German soldiers and short columns of captured Soviet soldiers. There were abandoned suitcases along the highway. At one point later on in our trip, I took some clothes for myself, as mine were all lost back at the abandoned trailer. I recall one blues dress with tiny red buttons, and one with flowery prints of red, blue, and yellow that I fancied. They were not nearly the quality of the ones I left behind, but they fit. I still had my good coat and kept it for years. I also had a scarf, which became multi-functional in the following few years, serving as summer halter top, bathing suit top, headscarf, and pretend blouse under a sweater.

The next fifteen or sixteen days appear in my memory as a montage of images, not necessarily connected or in any chronological sequence.

Early on in our journey, while we still had supplies, my mother and other women were invited into a farmhouse to prepare some foods to carry with us. The large kitchen was soon bustling with activity, while the steam from pots and the aroma of various breads baking in two large ovens filled the entire farmhouse. This idyll was abruptly interrupted by the news that the Soviet troops were once again closing in on us. All that was ready was hurriedly gathered, but a good portion of the unfinished foods had to be left behind. In the rush, my poor mother forgot her glasses. She was farsighted all her life and now she was forced to go without her specs for a long while.

This was the last time we had a near encounter with advancing troops. My guess is that the main thrust of the invasion was going to Vienna and when our group took a turn north to upper Austria, we got away from their path. Along the way, we passed many empty homes, and even towns, that had only a few people left. We stopped one night at an inn that was also a mill with a large wheel overlooking a rapid alpine brook. The owners were the only occupants and they did take our paper money that was pretty soon totally without value. For all I know, they knew it.

Almost without fail, the Austrians were kind and helpful to us even though they too were in great danger and had very little. One particularly fond memory involves standing on yet another farm amidst barns and corrals and piles of manure. A woman was milking a cow. When she finished, she poured a glass full of the still warm milk and handed it to me. Nothing ever has or will match the magic of such happiness. By this time, most of our food was gone and we often contented ourselves with eating frozen potatoes we dug from the thawing fields around farms. We ate once a day after we found the place to settle for the night. More often then not, we slept in barns on beds of straw. I, and probably everyone else, would fall immediately into a deep sleep. Once our group separated from the main road caravans, we were often allowed to spend the night in the traditional parlors of farmhouses. They were all spotless and exactly alike, with built-in wooden benches in one corner around a large square table made of dark wood polished to a brilliant shine. In another corner was a built-in ceramic or earthenware stove. We did get out of the cold Austrian spring weather, but I don't recall that these rooms were heated. We slept on the floor. Thank goodness for outhouses, I say to this day. We usually washed our hands and faces in the ice cold water of an alpine brook

For some people, walking all day and eating very little was very try-ing, but five or six of us kids continued banding together as we did in the pensione and managed to play games and continue our friendships and quarrels on the road as teenagers do everywhere. We usually outstripped the adults, and on one particular afternoon, we were sitting on a hill overlooking the highway when we spotted a truck with two Wehrmacht soldiers driving by. The truck bed was loaded with large, brownish round objects. "They are carrying footballs," someone exclaimed. One of the "balls" at that moment fell to the ground, and when the truck was well out of sight, we all ran down the hill. Imagine our surprise to find a large round loaf of bread. Triumphantly we presented it to our parents when they arrived and we all had food for almost three nights.

At one point, my mother was invited by a family with a horse drawn carriage to ride with the driver because her feet were badly blistered. I walked next or behind the wagon and tried to communicate with their kids. There were all kinds of people from all kinds of countries. All sorts of Slavic languages could be heard, interspersed with Hungarian, Romanian, and the international communicational broken German.

There were a few scary episodes as well. Shortly after my mother lost her glasses, we came upon a clearing in a forest teeming with a sea of humanity. People, speaking in strange foreign languages, were milling around everywhere. Amidst the confusion and noise, we suddenly lost Mommy. It was near dusk and George, holding me tightly by the hand, began going around looking for her. He acted with his usual calm, yet his somber manner told me he was very worried. It seemed like an eternity before she finally emerged from the early evening mist.

On another fine day, walking along a highway between rows of tall slender pines, we heard the approaching sound of small, low flying airplanes and the rat-tat-tat of machine gunfire. It meant a strafing was coming, and we ran among the trees and threw ourselves on the ground. Someone pointed up to the trees. They were all perforated by bullet holes from previous attacks. I heard the droning of the planes and the rat-tat-

tat getting closer and saw the plane with an unfamiliar insignia coming toward us at an angle when my parents covered me with their bodies. I was sure this time that we were all going to die. They would be shot and I would suffocate under them. The flyers must have realized they were shooting at refugees, or maybe they just wanted to have a bit of fun. In any case, they left after one pass. We dusted ourselves off and got back on the road.

The curious thing is that I cannot recall one moment of overt display of emotion by anyone during those days. It wasn't that people acted like zombies or appeared dazed or in major shock. It just seemed that this was neither the time nor place to waste energy with high drama.

There was one exception to this for me—the day we got in the way of an air raid and found refuge in a cathedral in a huge cave of a mountain. I was told that we had thousands of feet of rock on top of us and that we were totally safe. The interior of the cave was very beautiful with an elaborately gilded altar, frescos, and all the appropriate Gothic trappings. To this day, I cannot say exactly what came over me, but as I leaned on a carved wooden railing, I gave myself over to an ocean of tears, allowing them to flow freely and to wash away all the pent up anxiety and stress that must have been building up within me, perhaps ever since I unlocked the bathroom door on the day we left the old house. I am forever grateful that the others in the cave just let me be. When the raid was over and the tears subsided, I felt pretty good and a little sheepish. Once again, I dusted myself off and went on.

George finally had enough with all this wandering about the Alps. We were now definitely in what was to be the American Zone and he decided to join his brothers who were already settled in a small village just north of the city of Linz. So the three of us set off for the alpine village called Spital am Phyrn. In one of the towns, he bought railroad tickets, and we took a train stopping in Linz, where we spent one night sleeping in the station among homecoming soldiers. One of them let me use his legs for a pillow and shared his coat to partially cover me. During the night, blood seeped through his bandages and I had some of it on me. He assured me that he was just fine and I didn't cause it and surprised me by saying he was one of the lucky ones. Three years later I went with a neighbor to welcome her husband home from a prisoner of war camp in the Soviet Republic. A trainload of haggard old men in their twenties and thirties arrived and I knew what my soldier meant. But they too were lucky—most never came home.

Later we also learned that the railroad station of Linz during those days received one hundred consecutive nightly bomb raids with one exception. That was the night we spent there. The next morning we set off to our new home: Spital am Phyrn.

The two uncles and aunts, plus cousins, including Madge, welcomed our raggedy threesome with great jubilation. They took us immediately to their room at the Gasthof zur Post a typical Austrian hotel. My dirt-caked clothes were peeled off and I had a delicious, warm bath in a real tub in a real bathroom. I could have stayed there forever. Then they fed us spaghetti with a thin sweet sauce that made the three of us retch and sent us to the bathroom back and forth all night long, and since we all slept in the same room, uncle, aunt, and cousin, we had to step over them and thus kept everyone up half the night. In a few days, we could eat regular meals again. My cousin loaned me some nice clothes to wear, but when mine were cleaned I got back my little pleated school outfit to grow up in.

Spital am Phyrn

The spring of 1945 brought the end of World War II. For me, the day that marks the end of it is not the official Armistice Day but the one I witnessed somewhat earlier.

A tall Wehrmacht Major in black boots and riding breeches standing in the middle of the square was directing traffic with German precision. Behind him loomed the beautiful Baroque cathedral of the town, flanked by the wings of its adjoining abbey. The monastery had not been used for a long time, and although some of its rooms were already occupied by Hungarian refugees, most were unused. The town was nestled safely among its guardians, the snowcapped mountains of northern Austria. A highway came in from the south and continued northbound at the opposite side of the square. All the other roads were unpaved and it was obvious that no car or truck had any intention to take any of these, so it was a little unclear why the need to direct them, especially by a field officer, was necessary. Streams of vehicles of all types and sizes came and went through the town. Not one of them ever stopped. There was something so obviously futile in the officer's seemingly last ditch efforts, but he kept waving them on, perhaps to avoid the total loss of control or to hold back the inevitable. Nobody seemed to pay much attention. I was just passing by, but I keenly sensed the atmosphere of chaos and futility. So this is how this scene, etched on my mind, represents the end of World War II. Everyone knows or declares to know that war is a terrible thing, but sometimes I wonder if people fully comprehend the ridiculousness of it.

The pathos was heightened by the unrelenting beauty of the place. Fields carpeted with yellow daffodils, lush green hills sprinkled with crocuses, lilies of the field, and violets, brooks like rapids running wildly with the waters of freshly melted snow and playing peek-a-boo under the curved stone bridges throughout town, the lily ponds with their frogs, all performed their eternal spring ritual, unaware and uncaring of the ongoing human drama.

In a short while, the traffic went away, as did the officer, and the town returned to its usual tranquility. For a day or two, the square stood mostly empty. Then, one day as my cousin Claire and I walked into town, we heard an unfamiliar sound of motors approaching from the south. Then a jeep with four American soldiers came into view. The WWII jeep and the helmeted soldiers are recognizable throughout the world nowadays, but it was the first time I had seen such a sight. Claire, who was usually brave and coolheaded, turned around and ran away, but I stood mesmerized as the jeep followed by an entire convoy passed me by. They were alert and vigilant—these battle-weary men. This was not Italy where the population was jubilant, and where laughing girls threw flowers and kisses and jumped into jeeps. This was the heartland of an enemy country.

Nevertheless, some of them took note of the curious little girl standing on the dusty road and smiled and waved. After a while, I waved back.

Life Among the Bank People

Spital am Phyrn was chosen by the Hungarian National Bank as a safe place to store the Hungarian gold reserve. The Soviets had a habit of absconding with the national wealth of countries they invaded. It was for this reason that the management of the bank, which included my Uncle Julius as its chief legal officer, decided to find a suitable town deep within the pre-designated American Zone. A train with the gold bullion and large numbers of bank employees departed from Budapest long before our little family left there. Madge's father Uncle Andrew was also on the legal staff and although they were in Sopron with us for a while, they too soon joined the group in Spital. Sometimes this train is called the Gold Train, an unfortunate coincidence that leads to confusing it with the in-famous Nazi gold train that carried the treasures stolen from wealthy Hungarian Jewish families.

Once the war was over, the American government returned the gold reserve to Hungary with much fanfare so that the Soviets would not dare to touch it.

So there we were, George, Mommy, and I, guests of the Hungarian National Bank.

Our home for the next few years was a narrow room on the second floor of a wing of the U-shaped Gasthof zur Post just off the main square of Spital am Phyrn. Our window looked directly over a fast-flowing brook and we were never without the sound of rushing water, not even during the long Austrian winters, as these brooks ran much too fast to freeze over. I liked to stand at the window and watch the goings-on of our new neighborhood. If I looked to the left I had a good view of the square and its plentiful activities, and directly across over the brook I could look into the busy kitchen of our local bakery, the source of all good things. I was on a waving and smiling acquaintanceship with the baker family that sometimes had its rewards in an extra slice of bread on distribution day.

Once a week, the bank people would line up for their weekly bread rations. In some ways, the excellent quality of the bread was a hindrance, for it was almost impossible to resist gobbling it up right then and there. In fact, a couple of bachelors among our acquaintances did just that, reasoning that one good meal a week was better than a few morsels every day. The loaves doled out to families at least gave the appearance of something more substantial. The scarcity of food was difficult for some people. I don't recall ever being troubled by it, although now and then the image of trays of pastries that were laid out on the sideboard of the dining room of the old house back home would appear in my dreams.

Gradually, others drifted into the area as well, some individually and some in groups. Then a regiment of American soldiers arrived and filled up the old monastery. Just outside of town in old army barracks were many other refugees, notably pretty young wives of Hungarian Army officers waiting for their husbands who were in various camps as war prisoners. Some of these wives found temporary solace with the handsome group of American officers who lived in the luxury apartments of our inn. So the formerly tranquil hideaway of upper Austria was bulging with all types of noisy foreigners. An enterprising Hungarian jazz group soon found a place for a nightclub, there were dances and impromptu cabarets put on at the banquet hall of the Gasthof, raggedy theatrical groups would come through town, and although there was no food, the beer began to flow at the local pubs.

The lack of food was not high on my list of priorities, but I could not escape it entirely. Every midday a community meal was served in the dining hall of the inn, cooked by the wives of various bank employees. Madge's mother, who was quite undone by the general uncertainty of our situation, played a major role in the preparation of these meals and was known to skim some of the best parts of meats for her family. My mother, who never got her cooking wings, and who even after we arrived in the U.S. considered green beans in Campbell's mushroom soup to be haute cuisine, helped out only because of a sense of duty and with a bit of anxiety tinged by disdain for the goings-on. Young girls, such as I, were also expected to do their duty as kitchen maids. More often then not, we just over-peeled tons of potatoes amidst much bickering and sometimes hilarity in one of the anterooms of the crowded kitchen. Large quantities of bulk foods, like lentils and dry pasta, were brought from Hungary by the bank's train, but the supplies were running low after a while. We ate a lot of soup with small pieces of some animal and potatoes.

George and his brothers were great horsemen all their lives. The proudest moment of Uncle Julius' life was when he put his four-year-old daughter Claire on a favorite gelding and she sat on it like she owned the world. "What a seat she had," even George remembered. Before the war, Uncle Julius kept a stable at his summer place just up the Danube from Budapest. In the winter, his horses, along with the two owned by George and Uncle Andrew, were boarded in town until the big event each spring when the three brothers and their groomsmen would ride them to the summerhouse where every weekend large riding parties would assemble. These horses were called up for war service long before the end of the war and their unknown fate was of great concern and sadness to my uncle.

There were a few Hungarian horses that made their way to Spital, and although they were a sad lot and not the magnificent creatures of Uncle Julius' stable, they too were special to the brothers. But the horses could not be fed, so one by one they had to be slaughtered. Horsemeat is not too different from beef and tasted pretty good, as did the blood pudding George cooked up on the pot belly stove in our room, especially with the accompaniment of wild mushrooms provided by Mommy, who found someone who knew how to pick the edible, non-poisonous kind.

The nearby woods were a veritable herb garden for those in the know, but the only fruit trees were ones with tiny, very sour green apples that could not be eaten raw but made a mean and powerful cider. Since there was no sugar to be had, making jams or jellies was out of the question. A favorite and rewarding pastime was to go raspberry picking. One afternoon, Madge and I, equipped with large cans made into buckets with wire handles, wandered way up the side of a mountain, finding more and more abundant raspberry bushes. We had our buckets half filled when we began to hear strange long whistles. We stopped to listen. Silence. Lost in our work and talking most of the time, it was a while before we heard it again. This time when we stopped, I put my finger to my mouth and as we listened more attentively, we heard the whistle clearly, then another, then another. The rumor that German soldiers were still hiding in the higher regions of the woods came to my mind, and as I turned around, I could see that we had wandered quite a ways above the town. I told Madge what I was afraid of, which scared her too, which in turn made my assumption real and lickety-split, we decided to run for it down the mountain, spilling raspberries in our wake. We arrived back home quite breathless and we dramatically related our story, only to be informed that the deer that inhabited these woods made a whistling sound to warn each other of danger. We preferred to think that we escaped from the clutches of wild, renegade Nazi soldiers. It made a much better story.

Long after the war, the population in Austria remained on the rationing system, and it was only after the Marshall Plan actualized and other world organizations arrived with help, and a viable and very active black market came into being, that the scarcity of food was not a daily problem. But even before then, babies got more milk, as did pregnant and nursing women, teenagers up to sixteen were issued cards for a cup or so of blue milk a week that could also be turned in for a small amount of other dairy products such as a pat of butter or bites of cheese, and men whose work was considered heavy labor got more meat and bread. Here in the heart of the lumber industry, there was a shortage of healthy young laborers, since most of them had to go of to war, so some of the men from the bank and the camp, including George, volunteered to become lumberjacks. The jobs didn't last very long, but while they did the men had a pretty good time—doing physical labor in the fresh alpine air helped to lift their spirits as well. The tough old Austrian warriors of the lumber world got a big kick out of watching these city slickers struggling with work that was second nature to them, all the while giving friendly advice and half-mocking encouragement.

Like a Weed

There was no school. The Austrians did their best to feed the hordes of refugees but could not open their schools to the scores of children who for the most part didn't even speak proper German. Mommy began to teach little children to read and write in our small room. She also began to teach me English. But basically most of us older children and teenagers were left to our own devices. "You poor little thing," Mommy said to me years later, walking on a sunny day on the Stanford campus, "you grew up like a little weed."

She was right. I did grow up like a weed. After we arrived in the United States five years later, I went to school day and night, summers and winters, and managed to graduate from high school at nineteen and go on to a good college. So academically I more than made up for those years, but I didn't get the same social development and discipline that children get during the day-to-day experience of a middle school. Neither did Claire or Madge, nor scores of other kids. Did we miss out on something? Sure we did. But, oh, we learned so much. Next time you go out in your garden to struggle with your stubborn weeds, think of me.

In my early teens, I had the notion that grown-ups were privy to some knowledge that I lacked and that once I became an adult, some magical door would open and I would know how to handle situations, my thinking and behavior would be correct, and the doubts and fumblings of daily living would evaporate.

I was the youngest of the three cousins. Claire, whom I idolized and whose every move I tried to emulate, was four years older than I, an enormous difference at the time, while today we are both old ladies in our seventies, and Madge, only a year and a half ahead of me, was a cool customer who in those days at least went around with a half-smile on her face, almost a smirk, and nothing seemed to ruffle her feathers. Although I spent a lot of time in their company, neither relationship ever got warm and cozy.

Our mothers were very different also. Their mothers were much more domestic than my mother, who was bookish, loved taking long, solitary walks in the countryside, and was more comfortable with the interesting people with whom George always managed to surround himself than with an unruly teenager. It wasn't that she didn't love me. "It's terrible how much I love you," she'd say to me often towards the end of her life. I thought it was an unfortunate choice of words, but nonetheless I appreciated them and now that I am getting on in years too, they bring tears into my eyes. But Mommy was of a world where parents turned their ten-year-old daughters over to the care of some expensive institution and didn't pay much attention to them until in eight years they emerged culturally and socially polished, with excellent manners and the ability to dance well with any eligible tuxedo. And there in Austria with an uncertain future, sick with worry for her parents who were now in the clutches of a sadistic regime, her past in ashes, Mommy too was waiting for a magical door to open before her.

So I fended for myself as best as I could. For a while, I ran with the older crowd, managing to get myself into several embarrassing situations in my eagerness to be grown up. I began taking the cigarettes offered and took inhaling lessons usually until I got so dizzy and nauseated that I had to go back to our room, where I claimed a stomach ache. Poor Mommy worried about my frequent bouts, but I persevered and my "stomach trouble" miraculously disappeared as I became accustomed to smoking.

I regularly attended dances Saturday nights at the ballroom of the inn, and many private dancing parties in smaller rooms arranged by the Hungarian young people. We pooled our records and played the same old tunes over and over again on a portable phonograph with a manual crank that was in need of frequent and temporary repairs. I fell in love on a regular basis with one young man after another, often embarrassing them as I put my head on their shoulder with an adoring gaze when they asked me to dance. Usually they never asked me again. When I knew better, I was mortified by the memory of such lapses of judgment, and it wasn't until I understood what it means to be a budding girl without guidance in society that I forgave myself.

After a while I gave up on finding true love among the Alps and began to enjoy myself running with a younger group of girls and boys. It was a lot more fun going with this group. Now and then we would take a train to a nearby town called Hinterstodel that had a movie house. The train wound itself along high and narrow precipices and we had to go through three tunnels before reaching our destination. It was during one of those infrequent trips that I saw my first film in full color, the German-made magical fantasy called *The Adventures of Baron von Munchausen* that so impressed me that I can vividly recall certain scenes to this day. After the movie, we usually had some postwar concoction resembling sorbet in an ice-cream shop before we took the train back.

In the short summer, on more than one occasion, we did manage a torturous climb up another mountain to Gleinkersea, an alpine lake that was reputed to be bottomless yet the warmest in the country. True as that may have been, it still felt as cold as ice on the first dip. Lacking a swimsuit, I fashioned a bathing outfit from a pair of shorts and a scarf that I learned to secure very carefully, as the first time I wore it one side fell open and I exposed one of my puerile breasts. I can still see the look on a boy's face when this happened, and here was another mortifying incident that took me forever to get over.

All this time, I continued in my resolve to stop chasing young men. And, as it so often happens in life, it was in the letting go that I found. One day my friends and I were sitting around on the grassy side of a hill dappled by the August sunlight while nearby the American soldiers were eating their lunch. The chow line was in the courtyard of the inn, set on a series of long tables. That particular day, some of them sat near our group and we checked each other out for a minute or two. After a while, some of the boys in my group started a friendly kind of ruckus and as we got quite boisterous, I noticed one of the soldiers watching me with half a smile and obvious interest. I have to admit I played it for all it was worth and that evening my mother was surprised at the eagerness with which I applied myself to the English lesson. In the next few days, the soldier's and my paths crossed again several times and we finally struck up a conversation as best as we could. I found out his name was Bob Stober and that he came from Breckenridge, Texas. He was about twenty years old. I knew these young men had seen combat, but he was most gentle and much kinder than the self-conscious and self-absorbed young men I fancied at the dances. I found myself really liking him. It didn't hurt that he was exceedingly handsome. Then one afternoon when I came back to the hotel, I was told that the troops were leaving that evening. The trucks were already lined up along the street in front of the arched gate of the inn. I ran from our room as fast as I could down to the courtyard. Dusk was descending rapidly, but I saw him standing at the inner corner of the gate looking around searchingly. His face lit up when he spotted me. I ran toward him and he grabbed me and held me very close. I knew I was going to get kissed for the first time. I closed my eyes and offered my mouth to him. What followed took me by surprise. A kiss was much more than I had imagined—I gave myself totally to the pleasure of this new sensation until one of his buddies pulled him away and he jumped on the last truck. We didn't wave—we just kept eye contact with each other until we faded from each other's view. That evening, I looked at my face in the mirror, trying to see if the miracle that happened had left its visible mark and if other people could perceive the great change that took place that day in me. I don't remember that I missed him—I may have—I know I never cried, nor did I carry on about it. I just locked Bob Stober and those precious last moments with him away in my heart forever. It was never like that again. I wonder sometimes nowadays if there is an old man somewhere in Texas who now and then thinks of the girl in a faded short school skirt and long chestnut hair he kissed on a cool Austrian summer evening.

I bet he does. I hope he does.

The Cathedral

My cohorts and I liked to explore the cathedral and the nooks and crannies of the monastery. We were particularly fascinated by the piles of skulls of long deceased monks stacked neatly in pyramids behind iron bars in the alcoves on the outside perimeter of the cathedral. Sometimes we'd climb up one of the two bell towers and sit with our feet dangling on the outside, look around the countryside, yell at people below, or just enjoy a spitting contest. It was exceedingly dangerous, but exhilarating. Other times we just walked around the interior of the cathedral among its gilded splendor, examining the details of the frescos, strolling along the Stations of the Cross, and whenever someone was playing, listening to the music that emanated from the magnificent organ. If George or Uncle Andrew were playing, I would often help out with pumping the bellows. I loved it all.

The cathedral served various purposes. Many people, of course, found solace attending Sunday Mass or just sitting or kneeling quietly, praying and meditating in one of the pews at any given time of the day. Others found very different delights. My step-cousin, young Andrew, now almost a man, for example, used one of the upper balconies for his numerous dalliances. Hidden behind the huge marble columns, he exchanged passionate kisses and took other liberties with more than one pretty young woman. Andrew could always be counted on for high drama. A young woman of Armenian descent from the officers' wives camp, a few years older than he, was his first conquest. She got pregnant. An abortion was performed somewhere in the inn, after which, as two men carried her on a chair across the courtyard, Andrew followed the procession, wailing at the top of his lungs, "They killed my child," thereby announcing to practically the whole world what had just taken place. I was watching this spectacle from a window on the upper corridor along with some of our more curious neighbors. The unfortunate young woman left town shortly after that, and, since Andrew was so charismatic, soon other young ladies succumbed to his charms. Eventually he fell hard for the one girl who I thought was the least attractive of the lot. Her family was among those few who chose to return to Hungary, and Andrew went with them. This decision eventually culminated in disastrous consequences for him. Mary was long forgotten when years later he got caught in the 1956 uprising, imprisoned, and mercilessly tortured before he was finally released. He then managed to re-cross the now heavily guarded border to the West and eventually settled in British Columbia, where he continued pursuing and conquering as many women as he could. But some of the old savoir-faire was replaced by a benign but chronic bitterness.

Just about the time that Andrew was enjoying himself on the upper tier of the church, Claire began her vigil in the pews among the gilded woodwork and pastel frescos, lit by the rays of the sun that shone through the high stained glass windows of the cathedral caressing the honey colored tresses of her bowed head or glistening briefly on her tear-soaked cheeks whenever she lifted her face. This was not theater. This was genuine supplication for the safety of the father she adored. In August of 1945, Uncle Julius was arrested by the American authorities, shackled, and after a short incarceration in a concentration camp near Salzburg, extradited to the puppet Hungarian Communist Government. In a very short while, this type of cooperation ceased between the Western and Eastern Allies, as the true nature of the Soviet agenda became more apparent and the first signs of the now famous Cold War manifested themselves, but for a while the two powers worked in tandem. He was then flown to Budapest and put immediately into the infamous prison on the corner of Andrassy and Marko Streets. His trial was held in March of 1946. The charges against him were twofold. He was sentenced to six months on a charge that he made derogatory remarks against the Red Army, whereby he aggravated the postwar cooperation between nations. The second charge was that by holding on to a leading position at the bank as head of the Judicial Department of the National Bank of Hungary even under the Arrow Cross regime, he contributed to the fascist government's ability to hang on to power in Hungary. This charge was considered a war crime. Mercifully and justly so, on this charge he was found not guilty and was shortly released from prison.

In Spital, our family was ostracized by many as a consequence— some out of fear and some out of pure enjoyment that probably sprung from long held grudges and envy. Incredibly, it was the known Nazi party members who avoided us like the plague and some would even cross the street to do so. Uncle Julius' former chauffeur, who was now a big shot on the black market, gave me a triumphant look one day that unmistakably conveyed, "Now I am somebody and you are not." I thought it ridiculous and sad at the same time in a sudden attack of maturity. I was learning a harsh yet necessary lesson about human nature. Of course, we had many friends whose loyalty remained unaltered. Nevertheless, Claire and her mother thought it better to move from the hotel and took a couple of rooms in a farmhouse on the outskirts of the town. I never heard the matter discussed and for me it remained shrouded in mystery until Claire told me the story when we were both grown up. George and Uncle Andrew worried and were very somber for a long time, particularly until they found out about the sentence, for during the postwar hysteria, hastily formed governments under the Soviet yoke were hanging people left and right on the most ridiculous trumped up charges.

Upon his release, Uncle Julius managed to escape back to Austria within a few months. George went to meet him in the French Zone for a day or so. The family went to France for a year or two, from where they eventually immigrated to Ontario, Canada. There Uncle Julius found a position with the Bank of Canada due to his former relationship with the Bank of England. Upon his retirement, he was decorated by the Governor General of Canada, an appointee of Queen Elizabeth, at a white tie gala specifically given in Uncle Julius' honor. He lived out his life in relative peace in Toronto, enjoying leisurely horseback rides with his daughter as long as his strength remained. In the last decade of the twentieth century, a reunion of the Gold Train people was held in Budapest and Uncle Julius was posthumously vindicated and honored by the Hungarian government for saving the gold reserve for his country.

A New Pair of Skis

Usually the brief Austrian summer gave way to a glorious autumn by early September. In the lower elevation of the mountains, the leaves began to turn and for a time the countryside was bathed in a gold-tinged array of colors, then the trees stood bare for a moment before the first snows of the long winter arrived around late October. Most of the high peaks surrounding Spital were snow-covered even in summers, but now the layers thickened and soon, sparkling new snow, whiter than white, systematically covered every inch everywhere. This was the country where alpine skiing was invented, and every child, as soon as he could stand, would have a sled or a pair of skis. Spital was not among the famous and fashionable resorts—there were no chalets, no ski lifts—but people, many from the nearby city of Linz, came by trains with their skis for the weekend or even just a day. On weekdays, however, the hills behind the inn were deserted.

I considered myself a pretty good skier, and one sunny afternoon I borrowed someone's well-worn second set of skis. I had brand new, lace-up, high ankle boots made by a local cobbler for my ever-growing feet, the only pair of shoes I owned, and I decided to have a go at it. I chose one of the slopes I thought I could navigate with ease. Unfortunately, the gently rolling Buda hills were no match for even the most gentle curve of an Alpine slope, and as I was picking up speed, which at first I enjoyed, I realized that at the end of the field there was quite a drop, but when I tried to stop myself, I just kept on going. So, being a fast thinker, I took my only choice and threw my whole body down and after a small slide came to a full stop pretty close to the edge. When I looked up, I could see a boy about sixteen, with the yellow hair and clear blue eyes so common among the local population, leaning on his ski poles with a big grin on his face. That was quite a maneuver, he seemed to be saying. I had seen him at a few of the dances and knew his name was Rudi. I scrambled to my feet—he sort of helped me, still laughing a little. "Come on," he said, "let me show you how to come to a stop." So we went back up a way. Saying, "Now watch me," he glided down a few feet with ease and confidence. He stopped, glided, stopped again. "Now you try it," he called to me. I did and on the third try I did okay but not well. "Of course you have terrible equipment," he told me. After he thought for a moment, he asked me to meet him one afternoon in a few days on the same hill. "Don't bring skis," he said before we parted.

On the appointed day, I found myself very excited and a little nervous before our rendezvous. Mommy asked me to return something to Claire's mother, whose house was just near the top of the hill where I was to meet Rudi. So I took off early. When I got to the house, Claire opened the door and seemed a bit nervous. I had never seen their new place and asked if I could look around. They rented one of the bedrooms and a pleasant glassed in porch with a lovely view as their day room. I don't remember how, but soon it became apparent that Claire was giving a party that afternoon to her friends, some of my friends included, and chose not to invite me. I think she was surprised that I wasn't hurt and that I declined to stay. I didn't give it a second thought at the time, being excited about meeting Rudi.

Rudi was waiting for me. Waiting with a pair of magnificent skis that he strapped on my feet—thus we began our lessons. He was like a god on skis, maneuvering his way through the snow with such grace and elegance. It was a pleasure to watch him. Of course, this small hill was child's play to him as he usually went to the steepest, most challenging slopes in the highest mountains, but I think he enjoyed teaching me. He taught me turns, showed me how to pick up speed, to slalom, plus many other skills, and I was getting pretty good because although he only came with me two or three afternoons a week, I was totally obsessed and went out almost every day.

I cherished those skis and carried them into our room. Mommy and George never noticed that they were not the borrowed, worn-out pair, and didn't understand why I had to have them by my bed. "She's guarding her skis with her life," I heard my mother say to a friend one day.

In the meantime, George went to Linz and found employment for all three of us with the Americans. He was to go first and Mommy and I were to follow as soon as he was settled. Rudi and I spent a Sunday afternoon racing on a fairly steep hill he thought I could handle. He let me win once. He was proud of me. I had to return the skis to him and near dark we walked to his home, which was a rambling house with several small buildings, a big barn, and other signs of a wealthy farm. We walked on the main road with our skis slung on our shoulders, turned in the gate toward the barn, and leaned our skis against the door. It was evening, there was a gentle but steady snowfall, and the light from the farmhouse windows shone in wide streaks on the snowy ground. I thanked him. We stood very close to each other. The steam of our breaths mingled in the cold air. We never touched but there was palpable electricity in the air. After a while, I said I had better get going. "My parents," I said, rolling my eyes. He chuckled. "Mine too," he said. We parted and I walked home to the Gasthof.

A couple of years later, Mommy and I went back down to Spital for a short summer vacation. The town was now almost empty compared to its heyday of refugees and American soldiers. For sentimental reasons, we chose to take our old room at the inn. There were only a few other guests in the hotel—nobody we knew, but I found some old acquaintances in town. I asked about Rudi. I was told that the previous summer during a climb, as he was straddling a sharp rock formation and making his way from one mountain to the other, he was struck by lighting and fell 200 meters to his death.

I could not bear to go to our hill behind the Gasthof. Instead, I walked the length of the Linden tree-lined lane toward the railroad station and back again. I wasn't a little girl anymore—I was wearing penny loafers, a pale green sweater, and a tartan skirt that covered my knees—and my heart was breaking. I could hear it crunch like the thin layer of ice on the virgin snow under our boots when Rudi and I made our way to the slopes.

The Cathedral in Spital am Phyrn.

My home in Spital.

G.I. Willie and friends. I am on the first on the left.

Colonel James Avery and Family - Hester, Johnny, Dickie, and Baby Jim-Tom.

The DPs: Mommy, George, and I in my mini school skirt.

Fritzie in his French Foreign Legion uniform.

My DP ID Photo.

Linz

Sometimes I wonder if it hadn't been for Bob Stober and Colonel and Mrs. James Avery, I would have set my heart to emigrate to the United States with such unshakable determination. It was our good fortune that the first Americans we met were the very best, honorable, and kind people.

Field officers' families were arriving from the States and they were looking for servants for their households. The three of us were among the families who chose to try out for these jobs that were open only to refugees and not to the general Austrian population. Uncle Andrew, Madge, and her mother too came up to Linz, as did the Count and Countess Pejacsevics, good friends of my parents, with their little dachshund in tow. I wonder what the nice American wife of the Major thought when she first laid eyes on her new maid, a countess, who wore a full length fox fur coat, albeit a little shabby, a small, stylish hat, high heels, and carried a little dog.

In order to get these jobs, we had to have passport photos made and we went in a group to Hinterstodl to have them taken. Then we had to go to the American hospital in Linz for a physical examination, and I am sure a cursory background investigation was also necessary. In the hospital, I had an unfortunate attack of stupidity that could have jeopardized our chances. I shudder to think of it to this day. The doctors who went in and out of the waiting room were speaking German. Somehow I picked up on their conversation about someone who had some kind of venereal problem that they were dealing with. It was, of course, very unethical of them to be speaking of such matters in public. I knew absolutely nothing about sex except for what I heard other kids talk about, but I pretended to be visibly amused by what I was hearing. The doctors took note of this and called on Mommy to ask her permission to give me a thorough pelvic examination and have a "private" talk with me without her presence. I really wish my mother had shut me up earlier, but I am proud of how she fought with them to prevent such an outrage. By this time, I had dissolved into tears and turned back to being a little girl, which sort of made the doctors realize that they were mistaken, and so I had my throat and ears and lungs checked and I was declared a stupid little girl but fit for employment. We got the job. Mommy and I went back to pick up our stuff in Spital in gloomy silence. Mommy was not happy with her little girl.

George went ahead to Linz to meet with Colonel Avery and got the keys to the big house they were assigned in the affluent Froschberg district and the two men began waiting for their respective families. Mommy, who had by then forgiven me, and I came up to Linz for good.

The Averys were not yet in the house but expected any day. George prepared lunch for us. I best remember the canned Vienna sausages, bowls of fruit cocktail, and Pabst Blue Ribbon beer. No words can describe how absolutely delicious everything tasted after so many years of meager and tasteless fare. I was just enjoying myself then, but when I think now of the magical taste of every morsel, and how happily and proudly George treated his ladies, I cannot recall another more sumptuous or elegant meal in our lives. Who knows? Perhaps that first luncheon in Linz was the third and most compelling reason I wanted to come to the United States so badly.

So we began our lives with the Averys performing our assigned roles in the household according to our station in life. George, who had the marvelous ability to take on any job, whether it was as a young litigator, a lumberjack, janitor, or advisor to Congress, and lastly teaching at his beloved Stanford Law School, with enthusiasm and mark it with his particular creative brand, served as butler and chef to the Avery household. He and Mrs. Avery would confer in the study on Mondays surrounded by her cookbooks and related paraphernalia, planning the menu for the week. Then George would go to work and create his masterpieces. The Colonel once dared to mention that his upside down pineapple cake was the best he ever tasted and Mrs. Avery grudgingly conceded it was better than hers even though it came from her family recipe. The family adored George. One evening when the Colonel and Mrs. Avery came home early from a party, they found him playing a nocturne on the piano. They asked him not to stop and he continued to play for them while they made themselves comfortable in armchairs. It turned out Mrs. Avery was a fairly accomplished pianist herself, so now they had the love of music in common as well. After that, they often asked George to play something for them when supper was done and the kitchen was turned over to me for the final cleanup. Needless to say, my parents and the Averys remained lifelong friends and, when we were finally all living in the States, they often visited one another in various parts of the country.

I don't believe my mother enjoyed her job as much as all that, but she loved the kids and she kept the house spotless and performed all her duties diligently, often to exhaustion. She never really warmed up to Hester Avery until they were on more equal footing later in life. Hester did like to play the role of mistress of the plantation and that of the grande dame in spite of her rather ordinary appearance, but she was a good-hearted woman all the same.

I had the kids. I was nanny to the kids. I bathed them at night, dressed them in the morning, played with them during the day, read their little books to them, thereby learning more English, and fed the baby at night. The oldest was about five, already very handsome with bright red hair and snow-white skin dotted with freckles. There was something infinitely sweet about Johnny. He endeared himself to me forever when one night I went to check on him before I went to bed myself and as I arranged his covers I saw that he was still wearing his brand new pair of ski boots. I knew exactly how he felt and I gently covered him without touching his shoes.

Dickie, the middle one, was a little sullen, shy kid given to frequent temper tantrums. He was said to have been "difficult." The youngest, just over a year old when they arrived, was introduced to us as "the baby," which is what we called him from then on even after he graduated from Princeton no matter how much Mrs. Avery tried to have us use her pet name of Jim Tom for him. Even though Baby was my charge, he was hopelessly spoiled by my parents, who taught him Hungarian before he learned English. The whole family had to learn the Hungarian words for *water, bathroom, hungry,* and many others and continued to do so for a long time after they returned to Virginia. George believed that since Baby was the brightest of the three, the early education he received from us was what got him on the road to the Ivy League.

The older two had other friends and went places with their mother, but Baby and I spent most of our afternoons hanging out. I took him for long walks visiting my friends in the neighborhood, and sometimes we'd ride the bus that served the USFA (United States Forces in Austria) community into the city and back without getting off just for the fun of it. In the evening, I cooked his cereal in the bustling kitchen, among George's and Mommy's pots, and fed him in his highchair in the anteroom between the large kitchen and dining room. I always had to add a half a cup of water to the cereal the last few minutes; once I saw that my mother had put the water already on the stove. Baby ate his dinner as usual, leaving a spoonful or so, which I generally ate myself. This time it tasted peculiar. Then I found out that in order to cut down on the smell of the cauliflower Mommy was cooking, she put some vinegar water on the stove, which is what I poured on the cereal. I waited for Baby to get sick, but he never did and I never saw the need to share this information.

Mrs. Avery was appalled at the condition of my shoes, and since we had the same size feet, she immediately gave me a pair of sandals and some saddle shoes. After a while, a huge Sears and Roebuck catalog arrived with a beautiful lady in an elegant white dress with black flowers wearing a large brimmed black hat on the cover. Mrs. Avery loved it so much she promptly ordered the whole ensemble for herself and when it arrived, the package also contained two pairs of shoes, one penny loafers, a Royal Stuart plaid skirt, and some other necessary clothing items just for me. My parents weren't home when all this arrived and although I was too shy to thank the Averys properly right away, I proudly laid my new wardrobe on the bed in our room on the third floor servant quarters.

Whenever the family went away for weekends, I went with them to be in charge of the two older boys. Baby stayed with my parents to be spoiled to the max. In this way, I got to see many beautiful parts of Austria and stay in elegant hotels and country manor houses. Once I even got to watch from the second story staircase while pretty Austrian models paraded in the latest creations from the famous House of Geiger in the large marble hall below. Another time we stayed near Lake Gmunden, where my expertise in handling rowboats came in handy and they trusted me to take the kids out on the water. Johnny was a willing learner, but Dickie was often afraid. He was "difficult" I was often reminded—but as far as I was concerned, he was just a pain in the ass.

I didn't actually have a lot of direct contact with Colonel Avery, as his duties as a high-ranking officer often involved traveling throughout the American Zone and he was frequently away for days. In any case, my main job was to care for the children. The one time we spent some time together was the night the two older boys got very sick in the stomach, throwing up all over the place and running to and from the bathroom. Hester was away on a trip, and I heard all the commotion, so I ran down in my pajamas to the second floor where the kids' bedrooms were and together with their father took care of them, going from child to child, holding their heads, changing their pajamas and sheets, washing and cleaning, until finally by early dawn their distress subsided and both boys fell asleep. It was early dawn before I could return to bed, exhausted. The Colonel told both Hester and my mother what a great job I did. Unaccustomed to praise, I was both embarrassed and pleased.

I could say that I had a crush on him, but that would hardly distinguish him from most good looking men I ran across those days when I was somewhere between thirteen and fourteen, but I did have a certain affection for him, perhaps more as a father figure. George and I got along pretty well, but he was not very fatherly, while Colonel Avery in some ways reminded me of my grandfather back home whom I missed so terribly in those days in Austria, together with all that we left behind; my way of dealing with the anguish was to put it out of my mind and heart.

Only on some late nights before falling asleep would I allow the tears to come while I bit my arm so hard as to never to sob out loud and wake my parents. It was the way of our family to endure grief privately and it was only later in life I regretted that my mother and I never spoke of our feelings. Sometimes I had the impression that she thought I was void of deep feelings and other times her pain was so all consuming that I daren't approach her lest some unspoken nightmare would become reality and she would somehow disintegrate. It was just about this time that my mother and I began to grow apart, and although we continued loving each other, we never again became intimate until the very last years of her life. She lived to be ninety, so it took a long time.

On reflection I realized that Colonel Avery embodied all the qualities that attracted me to men throughout my life. I thought him sort of handsome and once I even told him as much in a roundabout way. One afternoon upon returning from seeing the movie *Gaslight* with Ingrid Bergman and Charles Boyer, I declared that Colonel Avery was the spitting image of Charles Boyer. He responded with the bemused smile he usually reserved for his kids, but I also detected a slight blush.

He was an intelligent, ethical man, honest to the core, and in his particular quiet good-natured way, was more likely to meet calamity with tolerance and a half smile than anger or overt disapproval. He came from an old, aristocratic Virginia family—most of his forbearers had distinguished military careers. One of his ancestors fought at Gettysburg. Following family tradition, he was a graduate of Virginia Military Institute. Both he and Hester spoke with that beautiful, melodious, cultured southern accent, much like the historian and writer Shelby Foote, which is almost totally unfamiliar to people in the western United States where many people think the south is populated with redneck Neanderthals.

As a grand finale to the Averys' tour of duty, they decided to give a grand dinner party for some very important people, including the General. What Mrs. Avery didn't know about formal entertaining George filled in for her, and so they determined to do it up right. George not only prepared an elegant feast, but actually dressed up as butler for the occasion, while I donned a black dress with a frilly apron and cap, as I was to serve the secondary dishes like vegetables, salad, and so on, while George presented the main fare and the appropriate wine he chose for each course. I practiced for days to learn all the right moves and correct sides from which to offer or take the used plates, and all sorts of intricate details of correct meal serving. It was magnificent theater. Upon arrival, the guests, the gentlemen in full dress uniform and their ladies in long evening gowns, were ushered into the main salon or living room for aperitifs and hors d'oeuvres. At the appointed time, George opened the double doors of the dining room to announce, "Ladies and Gentlemen, dinner is served," while I stood in my uniform and most serious face at the sideboard awaiting my big moment. When everyone was seated at the proper place, George closed the double doors, and the main show commenced. All went swimmingly. I did remember the proper order in which to serve each guest according to rank, although I forgot to offer one of the side dishes to the last person—the host—but he very discretely whispered it to George, who took care of it.

That being done, I went back to the living room to clean away the used glasses and dishes, empty ashtrays, open the window for a moment to air the room, fluff the pillows, and return to the dining room for the final phase of the supper. The evening was declared by everyone an astounding success, and Hester, George, and I glowed with satisfaction, even though I was a little mad at myself for forgetting to serve the host his veggies, but again all I got was the benevolent half-smile, and all was well after all.

It was a sad day when we had to say goodbye to the Averys, and soon we were to learn that not all Americans were as wonderful as they when we met the new tenant of the house. Quite the opposite, in fact.

Now For Something Completely Different

The house in Froschberg was assigned to another field officer whose family was not expected until several weeks later, so the three of us had the house to ourselves for a short time. We met the future occupant when he came to inspect his new quarters. He was a smallish, rotund, not very attractive looking Major, with a rather rough demeanor and a brusque way of talking, who had risen through the ranks due to the demands of the war. He arrived with an entourage that included a somewhat frumpy and cheap looking but pretty young Austrian woman who on acquaintance turned out to be a sweet natured and kindhearted little thing, a couple of sergeants, presumably his aides de camp, and even a private or two. Shortly after arrival, they settled down to the first of many boisterous drinking parties in the very room where only a month or so earlier the General, surrounded by ladies in shimmering evening gowns and their officers, enjoyed the caviar and pate canapés served on silver trays by the butler with a doctorate of law from Budapest and Berlin Universities. As Aldous Huxley would have said it: "Of such is the Kingdom of Heaven."

The irony was not lost on me, as I was already beginning to enjoy the peccadilloes of human behavior. Of course, I didn't know at the time that this kind of fraternizing the Major was engaged in was absolutely against Army regulation and highly inappropriate at best, nor was I remotely aware that our new employer and his cronies were engaged in some serious black market racketeering. Pretty soon the other men brought along their girlfriends and it was not unusual for one or two couples to go upstairs to a bedroom for a little tête-à-tête. After a while, the Major, who was generally very nice and fatherly to me, sometimes invited me to join a party. I was treated well and nobody ever made a pass at me, perhaps because my mother was in the house, or just because I was after all still a young girl. Since the little girlfriend, only a few years older than I, had become my friend, the Major encouraged me to accompany them on some excursions as her companion. Once we went to a fair and rode the Ferris wheel and other terrifying rides and walked down among the sideshows, but neither the girlfriend nor I wanted to see any freaks. The only "freak" we saw was the "fat lady" sitting in front of her tent, who, unfortunately for business, was just slightly overweight due to the famine of the war. She was about 145 pounds at most I would guess—not much of a show—yet for those times, a hefty piece of work nevertheless.

Most memorable was the grand finale of fireworks late at night, when after a while, the man who was in charge accidentally ignited his entire stock and it all went up at once, including the man himself. We didn't know that until later—we just thought it was a spectacular show. I commemorate the unfortunate man every 4th of July.

The Major allowed me to keep the corner bedroom on the second floor. Actually, I always thought it was the best room in the house, sunny and pleasant, with windows on two walls allowing views of both streets. I found some books about cowboys in English and I began to read, first because I wanted to show off, then because I got interested, so my language skills were getting better and better. Having much more free time without kids to care for, I developed friendships throughout the neighborhood with other young people and had long philosophical discussions and learned how to throw a ball properly from a young Hungarian acrobat who worked for the household next door and who went on to fame and fortune on Broadway. I also had enough money for an occasional movie and had fallen seriously in love with Jimmy Stewart.

Poor little girlfriend cried her eyes out when she was told that the Major's wife and two sons were arriving any day. If the Major ever saw her again, I never knew about it. George had had enough very early in the proceedings and went to look for another job, but Mommy and I, not having many choices in those days, had to stay until he could find something better for us, so we prepared the house as best as we could to rid it of all traces of the goings-on. Then the family arrived. A sad lot to be sure. The children barely made an impression on me and for the life of me I cannot recall their names or what they looked like. They must have been somewhere between six and eight years old. One day, shortly after they arrived and before we had a chance to settle down, the Major's wife, all dressed in her finery, was picked up by some ladies to go to her first Officers' Wives Luncheon at the Officers Club in the beautiful villa overlooking the Danube where I had gone with the Averys many times and where Johnny, Dickie, and I watched the wonderful Geiger fashion show from the top of the grand staircase. The Major's wife returned a crushed woman. I never understood why the other wives did this humiliating thing to her in such a manner even if they felt the need to enlighten her to as to her husband's unsavory and illegal activities. It's unclear what they knew or how much they actually disclosed. Except of course for the girlfriend, Mommy and I had no clue either in what he was engaged. The storm that followed when the Major came home that night was of hurricane proportions. Then an unbearable pall descended upon the house.

The Major's wife returned to the States. We never found out what became of the Major.

Spallerhoff

In the meantime, George was fortunate enough to find work as a lawyer with the Americans and was living with Uncle Andrew's family in another part of Linz called Spallerhoff—much less attractive than the lush hill overlooking the Danube where we had lived so far. Until George could manage to find a suitable place for us, Mommy took a job with a young American family just across from the Averys' house, and, for the time being, I too was parked at Uncle Andrew's house—and got to share a bed with Madge again. My journey had come full circle.

Uncle Andrew was the "super" of a big gray box of an apartment house divided into three sections, with small one or two bedroom flats on either side of the staircases on every floor. Each three floor section had a spacious attic with several storage areas, a privy, and a large cement laundry room with washing tub and potbellied stove for heating water. There were no elevators. The ground floor had a drugstore on the corner, a butcher shop in the middle, and a tobacco and newspaper store on the other end. The entrances to the staircases were located in the back of the complex off of a large paved area that also had a loading dock for the butcher shop and enough space for a car park for the residences. Only the few American tenants, non-coms with European brides, had vehicles. There was little vegetation behind the low concrete wall that surrounded the property. All was very utilitarian and sparse.

Spallerhoff was the heart of the large industrial section of town and many of the factories that kept Linz going through the war stood empty, as did the large gray buildings that housed the blue-collar force. A few workers remained in the area—most of whom were repatriated German families from various neighboring countries. I don't know what type of work they were doing, nor do I know when or what the complex was eventually renamed, but in those days the factory was still known as the

Goeringwerke among the locals even after Hitler's infamous henchman, Hermann Goering, was convicted as a war criminal.

For the time being, Uncle Andrew was entitled to one of the flats in our building. George and I and a few stray Hungarians who happened to pass by came to live with them. George shared a room with a very nervous and fussy man named Simon. Simon and Madge's mother ran the household and often had noisy disagreements mostly over meals. We were beginning to get food packages through the Marshall Plan—cans of a strange yellow spread called margarine, large tin boxes of broken crackers, some sweet, some salty, powdered milk, and occasionally even sugar. The butcher from the shop below always added a little extra to what our ration cards allowed. Aunt M was very frugal with their cards and doled out small portions to her brood. George, who was seldom around, didn't care. He gave me my sheet of stamps and I took the lot and went shopping for some delicious thinly sliced ham, a few pats of sweet butter from our friend the butcher, then walked over to the baker's shop just in time to see them take out the freshly baked Kaiser rolls. They'd cut them in half for me and I would fix myself a heavenly sandwich that I ate sitting on the side of our dismal courtyard. Sometimes I used up all my stamps this way.

I tried as much as I could to keep away from Uncle Andrew, who was often ill tempered and obviously disapproved of almost everything I did. Aunt M was unfortunately suffering from all sorts of anxieties about the shortages of food and the lack of other materials things. The one time she seemed to be relaxed and happy was when on a blustery afternoon, while sitting on the low concrete wall of our courtyard, she and I shared a few mugs of hard apple cider. For once neither of us was daunted by the severe glances from Uncle Andrew. And, as in Spital, Madge and I got along fine but never became really close friends. Fortunately this living arrangement was of short duration. Eventually Mommy left her job in Froschberg and we found a place of our own in the first section of the apartment building

Linz, a large economic center and industrial city, the capital of Upper Austria, is bisected by the Danube, which widens there after emerging from its narrow passage through the Bohemian forest into the Linz basin, and for a long time was the first major port of the shipping industry of the mighty river. In my day, the eastern side of the Danube was in the Russian Zone and we, as refugees, or for that matter the Americans, were not allowed to cross over. Not that I wanted to. In fact, I was terrified to even go near the bridge. Thus, whenever I rode the streetcar, I was always careful to get off two stations ahead and walk the rest of the way to the large swimming complex by the river, where I spent a good part of my last two Austrian summers lest accidentally the streetcar would forget to stop and carry me into the enemy's hands. Austria ostensibly was then divided into the four zones—American, Russian, French, and English—but as everyone knew, only the Russian and American Zones were of importance. To some, almost imperceptibly, and to others such as Winston Churchill quite predictably, the Cold War began in earnest. Finally the Americans began to acknowledge what any Polish, Hungarian, or Czech person could have told them; the Russians were up to no good. We had enough news through heavily censored letters and tales told by recently arrived escapees that the yoke of the new communist regimes was felt by everyone behind the not yet infamous Iron Curtain. My grandparents urged us not to come home. I believe Mommy wanted to go home because she longed to be there for them, but George listened well and knew better. For a while this caused a chasm in the marriage as well, so the atmosphere both in the world and at home was very tense. I wanted to go to the United States.

Of course, I cannot take credit for the final decision, except for my dogged and highly vocal determination to say no to Venezuela, England, or Australia, and certainly to Argentina where all the Nazis were going. George even had an offer from a university in the newly formed Pakistan and he promised me my own elephant and a little boy in a turban to follow me around and fulfill my every wish.

At the time, George was working among a group of Hungarian and American lawyers in downtown Linz. Most of the people who worked for the Americans were refugees from the surrounding nations. Each American lawyer was teamed with a European counterpart and worked primarily on civil cases arising from the occupation. George's partner was James Broly, an exceptionally intelligent, easygoing, southern drawling lawyer from Durant, Oklahoma (Brown County, he'd add). The two of them became very good friends, and Mommy and George often got together with them, and I sometimes babysat their little child. Mrs. Broly was writing an article about Austria and hoping to publish it in *Life* magazine. I don't know if she ever did. It was her father, the Lt. Governor of Oklahoma, Cowboy Pink Williams, who initiated our coming to the States.

In this respect, we were very lucky. Austria at the time was bursting with refugees. The country was peppered with DP camps; people lived in the basements and attics of apartment houses, some in abandoned railroad cars; there were apartment houses full of people released from concentrations camps, all trying to decide where to go to start a new life, and more importantly, who would take them in. Free countries all over the world opened their doors to these refugees. The most coveted, of course, was the United States, and after President Truman signed the 1948 Displaced Persons' Act, Mommy, George, and I were soon selected because the Brolys paved our way by finding us a sponsor, the First Presbyterian Church of Oklahoma City, and by guaranteeing a job for George.

In addition to those of us who left our countries during the last years of the war, hordes of people escaped daily from the Communist-occupied countries through the increasingly heavily guarded borders. And yet, now and then, through the intermittent show of good faith, the Soviets were releasing some prisoners of war, and trains with haggard Austrian ex-soldiers, some blackened forever by the coal mines, arrived at the railroad station.

There was even a DP Hospital near our home with makeshift temporary buildings, much like barracks, but equipped with an operating theater, examining rooms, a few wards, and some necessary medical equipment, plus an excellent staff because all the best refugee doctors assembled there—so much so that the young American doctors of the Military Hospital, and even some Austrians, would come there for advice and consultation or sent patients for diagnosis or treatment.

The head surgeon was a world famous Polish doctor who, I was told, was a morphine addict, which made him terribly glamorous to me. One or two of the Hungarian doctors were friends of George from back in Budapest and we socialized with them frequently. These men, some of whom had families, and some not, for whatever reason took me under their wing. I don't know if the care was free to everyone but it certainly was to me. Once, when I had something wrong with me, I saw one of the Hungarian doctors who seemed to look at my chart for quite some time. "Kostka," he said. "Your name is Kostka. Are you by any chance related to Istvan Kostka?" "Yes," I replied, "he was my father." "You don't say. Do you know that I was the doctor who treated the man your father shot? He died in my room at Rokus Hospital." I became famous.

The happiest day of my life was the day Uncle Andrew, Aunt M, and Madge left for England. By this time, they had to give up their apartment to some new American families and moved into one of the wash kitchens in the attic of the complex. When Mommy returned home we took another, smaller wash kitchen in the first section of the building. The first night was a nightmare of bedbugs and filth. So when the relatives left we got the bigger washroom, with extra room for a cot for me in the main attic, and some real furniture, plus a floor length mirror, and best of all, a radio. But just being without the scrutiny of Uncle Andrew was a blessing in itself. We accompanied them to the train station not only to say a tearful goodbye, but, at least for my part, to make sure they got off all right.

A new life began. The legal department was phased out, the Brolys returned to the States and George got a new job with an American agency, actually the precursor of the CIA, interviewing newly arriving people from the Communist block. As in the legal department, he worked with an American counterpart. It was their job to ferret out potential spies and moles. The Cold War was in full swing. He worked with some spooky people, I have to say.

Mommy took a job in the apartment house with yet another young family, this time from Texas, who also had the officer's mother with them. It turned out I could not work full time because of my age, so with the exception of a few jobs house, baby, or dog sitting, I was left to my own devices. I more or less kept house, or rather wash kitchen, for the family, and cooked our evening meal, which more often than not consisted of leftovers Mommy brought home. She often cooked rice at her work and I concocted a sauce of the various spices and herbs we inherited from people who moved from the apartment house to another town or country. But most of my time alone I spent reading and listening to the U.S. radio station and perfecting my English. I also tried my hand at writing short stories, a hobby I actually started in Hungary as soon as I could write. I made my own clothes, remembering some of the tricks my grandmother taught me, but I had to do it by hand, so I did it while listening to Fred Allen, Bob Hope, or Fibber McGee and Molly. I also loved Country and Western music and became a huge fan of the new sensation, Hank Williams.

If I had the money, I'd walk a mile or so to the streetcar and take it downtown, go to a movie, visit friends, and sometimes visited friends and went to a café or now and then even a bar with them. The last two years in Austria turned out to be the happiest of my life.

With George's penchant for making friends, Mommy's skills as a charming hostess, and my burgeoning social skills, the grim laundry room, with its cement floor and whitewashed walls, was transformed into a regular "salon." No invitation was necessary after the first visit and acquaintances, at times bringing someone new, would frequently drop in. Some came for one evening only, on their way somewhere in the wide and increasingly welcoming free world, and some were regulars whose presence could be counted on almost every night. We covered the large, built-in cement laundry tub that stood in one corner with a wooden board and placed a large porcelain bowl just under the tap. Then we shielded it from view when not in use with drapery that I fashioned out of a paisley tablecloth. Pillows rolled in blankets served as backs for the cots. Strewn with a few small cushions, they became couches; however, most people preferred sitting around the mahogany dining table in the middle of the room. Some guests brought bottles of wine or something more serious. Mommy saved all the coffee grounds from her employers, and, as she did since she befriended the Army KP guys who saved the grounds for her in Spital, we just kept adding them to a large pot on the hotplate—by now we had plenty of sugar—and we became famous for our delicious coffee—a rare treat for some indeed. The aroma of coffee and cigarette smoke has always evoked in me a feeling of well-being and comfort—a home. Everybody smoked. Cigarettes were the most valuable commodity on the black market. They were bartered, bought, sold, and of course smoked. When the Averys returned to the States, they sent us a case of cigarettes since they were not allowed to send us money. Mommy gave me two cartons. I bought a pair of officer's silver pants, had them dyed black and tailored to fit me, and still had enough left over for smokes and some to share. Mrs. Avery, not being savvy to the intricacies of the game, sent Old Golds. I was quite put out at first. Brands mattered. Had they sent Camels or Lucky Strikes, we could have done better business.

Our domicile was no longer suitable for its intended use, so our laundry was sent out to be done by a woman who lived in a dumpy little DP camp within walking distance of the apartment complex. She was a warm-hearted peasant woman who wore a babushka, several billowing skirts, an apron, and her sleeves were always rolled up to the elbow due to her occupation. She was also my main connection to the black market. The source of all good things. The sugar lady. This was the time when prisoners of war, actually slave laborers, were released from the Soviet Union, and more and more of them showed up from behind the Iron Curtain. Her daughter was one of them. She spent her years as a prisoner somewhere in the Ukraine and had quite a story to tell. She brought a chunk of dark tasteless bread and a pair of crudely made shoes with paper soles to show under what conditions she had lived. She said, as many others, that in some way the prisoners were better off because the local people in that wretched decimated country didn't even have an idea of how things could or should be.

A Night at the Opera

The last few years we lived in Austria before emigrating to the United States, life was beginning to return to its former style, albeit food was still scarce, many buildings still lay in ruins, and the scars of the devastation of the recent years were visible pretty much everywhere—but so were the efforts of restoration and rebuilding. The atmosphere was permeated with a new vibrancy infused with a sense of hope.

Theaters were opened and although the costumes may have been a little tattered, the sets a little shabby, the talent was not. My best beaux, Fritzie, took me to hear the *Tales of Hoffman* in the old Baroque Opera house of Linz. He made an effort to bring culture into my life. I believe secretly he felt my parents were neglectful of my continuing education. He was of course right, but since I didn't know what I was missing, I just enjoyed the freedom that he considered license to do as I pleased.

We had very good seats and in retrospect it must have cost him half a month's salary to take me. It was snowing when we left the theatre and walked to the streetcar station on the main square. I expected him to say goodbye there, but he got on with me. When we got to my station, he again surprised me by getting off and walking with me up the hill to Spallerhoff. I was in a giddy mood and began to dance in the freshly fallen snow, belting out parts of arias from Hoffman and occasionally stopping under the round spotlight of a street lamp for a dramatic, arms outstretched, finale of a high note. Fritzie seemed mildly amused, but by this time I knew he was totally enchanted by my antics. What I liked about our friendship was that I felt completely free to be my outrageous self with him whenever the mood struck me without fear of any reprisal.

After a while, I resumed a slower pace and we walked side by side until we reached the gate of the apartment complex. I put out my gloved hand and thanked him for a lovely evening. For a moment, we stood facing each other in silence. I wanted him to kiss me. He knew I did. I could tell he also wanted to, but then he thought better of it, and letting go of my hand, turned around and left.

Fritzie was so elusive. He fought so hard to avoid loving me. I was baffled and often frustrated, but for some reason never hurt. As it turned out it took a much more dramatic moment for our first kiss that eventually took place on the second landing of the stone steps of Spallerhoff project actually not too far from our non-kiss of the night at the opera.

The next cultural event we attended was the newly released film *Hamlet* with Lawrence Olivier at the Mozart movie house on Mozart Street, not too far from the Mozart Café. Fritzie and I held hands. My right hand that is—my left hand was fondled by a guy named simply Junior who was not an enigma and left no doubt as to what his intention was. If only looks could kill, I thought, whenever Fritz looked at Junior. I probably would not have given a second thought to Junior if I hadn't seen that look. What cruel fun it was to be sixteen.

On Our Way to Bremerhaven

From the back of a U.S. Army troop truck, I watched the snow packed road as it stretched out like a white ribbon (perhaps an umbilical cord) from under the heavy dual wheels and took us to a DP camp just outside of Linz. This was the first leg of our long and bumpy final phase of our Austrian years. It was the early winter of 1950. George knew a young Greek/Hungarian man who lived in the camp, and rather than staying in the dormitory to which we were assigned, we accepted his gracious offer to stay with him and his wife and child. At orientation next day, we discovered more friends, and from then on our trip was very social. In a day or two, we finally boarded a train and waited, sitting on wooden benches in the biting cold for what seemed, and may have been, hours, before we finally began lurching toward Salzburg. I had been there before but not in winter. Once in Salzburg, we again were assigned to barracks, a huge stone building. It looked like it was converted from a riding academy with its domed high ceiling, and the smaller rooms suspiciously resembled former stalls. It was so crowded and unbelievably unsavory looking that even after all the refugee years, we could not bring ourselves to settle there, particularly after we were informed that our stay would be of some duration. Spring planting was nearing in the U.S. and people who were going to work on farms were given priority for transportation. We had to wait our turn even before we could go to our port of embarkation—the German North Sea town of Bremerhaven.

So Mommy sold her last piece of jewelry, a slender gold pin with a single pearl and a tiny diamond. I remember looking at it for the last time standing on the sidewalk in the snow while my parents discussed their decision to sell. Somewhere a deal was struck, for soon we were ensconced in a tiny room in a cheap but clean little hotel very close to our barracks just below the castle on the hill that defines that famous town.

The hotel also had a pub-like restaurant on the first floor. Whenever we came down the stairs from our room, we passed by the open back door of the kitchen, from which delicious aromas tantalized our palates. I heard that plates of sausage and dumplings the size of baseballs were the most popular and sometimes only item on the menu. We never ate there because we were provided three good meals a day free at the large dining hall of the barracks. It was cafeteria, or chow line style, and we ate at long wooden tables with benches. Teenagers (I was not yet seventeen) got a somewhat more nutritious fare at designated tables—more vegetables, fruit and dairy products for growing bodies. Kids under twelve also had their own special tables. I soon made new acquaintances with people to hang out with here and there throughout the day.

In the evenings, I went with my parents to a family of friends who managed to rent a nice big room in a nearby villa. A lot of Hungarians had Austrian friends from even before the war who often extended hospitable courtesies. They didn't have food either, but at least some of them still had their house, or at least a livable part of it. It didn't appear to me that Salzburg was much bombed, but I learned later that about 40% of the town was either destroyed or damaged. Austria had a successful five-year plan of restoration for its cities and Salzburg must have certainly been one of the top priorities. It could also have been that everything was blanketed by snow, but unlikely, as my eye had seen a lot of snow-covered rubble by that time. Sometimes we played cards or parlor games, and when someone found a Ouija board we all checked out our futures amidst much hilarity. It was foretold that I would have five husbands in my lifetime. Caught up in the spirit of occult, once we even held a séance. It was all in fun, of course; at least, I didn't take it seriously and nobody else seemed to either.

No food was ever served at any of the numerous social events in which we participated throughout our DP years. Now and then we'd have coffee or tea, and spirits were frequently available. There was one constant though; the rooms were always filled with cigarette smoke. We did have our priorities.

It was usually late evening when the party dispersed and Mommy, George, and I walked to our hotel huddling together under dim street lights in the icy winter cold, the hardened snow crackling under our well worn shoes. I had a good winter coat, dark blue with fur collar, and underneath I wore the green turtleneck Fritzie literally gave me off his back when he came to say goodbye on his last visit before he left for France where he joined the French Foreign Legion.

I also spent a lot of time walking around by myself, enchanted by the mystical crystalline splendor of the snow-covered city. Once, crossing a bridge, I ran into a young Austrian man I knew from Linz, who, now fully restored to his aristocratic status, was coming from a skiing trip. At one time, he worked for George. I sensed he was rather haughty with me at this time; it may have been just my mood at the time, but I felt miffed nevertheless. When I told to George of our encounter later that day, his only comment was, "Freddie was always a jerk."

She is Leaving Home...

Another long and cold train ride, this time through Germany, commenced. I had never been in Germany before, and what I saw from the window of our wagon was a shock. That time of year—very early spring when the melting snow mixes with icy rain turning to mud during the warmer parts of the day and refreezing into grooves at night—has always been the worst time of the year in Europe. But it was more than that. Germany, unlike many other countries, and some would say deservedly so, wasn't recovering from the devastations of the war very well. Poverty, badly dressed people, rubble not yet cleared, and houses still showing the effects of bombing raids were everywhere. The towns as well as the countryside appeared void of color. The world from our windows was covered in a gray mist with only black and white images here and there. It's a fleeting but indelible memory in my repertoire of postwar experiences, but for the time being, I forgot it once we reached the camp at Bremerhaven where we were going to board our ship.

In the interim, we were housed in a large complex of well-built brick buildings originally built for crack troops of the Third Reich. The first order of business was a trip to the infirmaries to be dusted by DDT. We got no physical exams, as all the people had to be checked out medically before they could even enter the camp here. Only the healthy were eligible for emigration. The men and women had separate quarters. Mommy and I were assigned to one of several dormitories, each with large communal bathrooms gleaming with state-of-the-art showers, sinks, and toilets. We had a room with six beds. Most of our roommates were from the Ukraine. Each of us received a small bag with toothpaste, toothbrush, soap, a lipstick, and other such items. Many of the Ukrainian peasant women laughed about the lipstick and some of them gave them to me and some of them painted themselves and paraded mockingly. "Well, we're all Americans now," they'd say.

Since I was proficient in three languages, I was an official interpreter. It was a thankless job, except that I could make fun of it. The ones who knew a little German had no trouble, but as I spoke no Slavic language, their pleas in minimal broken German were hard to understand and harder to convey to the English speaking officials, some of whom spoke German as well as I did. All three of us, George, Mommy, and I, spoke English and so we were much in demand.

Meals were served in buildings with kitchens and large dining halls on long wooden tables with benches. We young people had our own separate dining halls. We were also provided with a sports and games hall, where we could enjoy basketball, Ping-Pong, and rooms for board games or music. I soon became a Ping-Pong champion, a game I learned way back in boarding school in Hungary, and thus became a special friend of the young German man who was our youth counselor.

Theo and I eventually became an item. He was very blond, very sweet, and very handsome. He was amused by my slight Hungarian accent and my Austrian German way of expressing myself. He thought I was cute, which to me was always irresistible. I was never given to hopeless love. I had to be admired and thought adorable before I fell in love. No flies on little Vivi one could say, but on reflection later on in life when I had gained some insight into myself and a bit of wisdom, I came to the conclusion that what I was looking for in these wonderful boys was the affection, the smiling indulgence, the pleasure they took in my being lively and interesting and finding my jokes funny, much like my grandfather did when I was a ensconced in the safety of his love as a little girl. To be sure, now the last European days I was sixteen, a month away from my seventeenth birthday, sported a thick mane of chestnut hair, had very nice boobies indeed, was said to have been built like a brick outhouse, and naturally all this appealed to most of the male population. But the ones I was drawn to and who caught my attention and affection were the ones who went beyond mere lust and saw the deep need I had for some serious and sincere affection and to whom I could show my vulnerability. I know this is what Fritzie responded to most, as I did in kind to his vulnerability and his loneliness. We were children who grew up too fast. Some of us never really settled down and could not successfully plant roots anywhere. The course of my generation was set by the total disruption of "normal" life by the very fate and geographic location of our homeland. Certainly a lot of damage was done, but I wouldn't give up one moment of it. I think in the long run we found something unique in the experience. I am unlike my contemporaries who stayed behind and grew up under Communism. They have another set of demons. The price was high. But I've always liked expensive things.

But back at the time in Germany. I didn't think my tryst with Theo was very serious and was surprised when on the actual sailing date he came to see me off. My mother was embarrassed and furious with me. Mommy and my boyfriends, with the exception of Fritzie, were always at odds with each other and not until my daughter became a teenager and this pattern was repeated did I realize that it wasn't my doing or fault. It was something Mommy could not handle for reasons best known to her. Theo looked miserable, to my great surprise. We shook hands. That's all that could be done. Then we were taken to the seashore, where I saw the great ship, The General Hershey, for the first time. It was smaller than I had imagined. I promised myself I would remember when I took my last step on the European continent onto the boarding plank, but I was distracted at the last minute and soon found myself onboard. This oversight bothered me very much until forty years later I went back and finally once again stepped on European soil.

We had a longer than usual, very rough crossing. The north Atlantic in March can be mighty fierce. Some people immediately got seasick. Mommy had a terrible gallstone episode that kept her down for almost the whole trip. Once we were out of the English Channel, even more people succumbed, and eventually it got so bad that one evening only George and I showed up at the mess hall for dinner. We were served a terrible concoction of eggs and fish, which to this day I am sure was designed to get rid of us too so the kitchen crew could be idle, but they didn't reckon with our fortitude and we continued to enjoy our meals while the salt and pepper shakers slid from one end of the long table to the other. I had good reason to be well after one particular woozy episode one day while still in the Channel. George suggested I go out to the deck for fresh air. A handsome young merchant marine, who had been watching me for days whenever I was sunbathing on deck with my friends before the weather turned, spotted me in a doorway. I was contemplating throwing up or throwing myself overboard when he offered me a cigarette, not noticing or perhaps choosing to ignore my distress. I girded myself, thinking, "This will either kill me or cure me," as I took the world's longest Pall Mall and bent over his cupped hands for a light. By the time the Pall Mall was extinguished so was my seasickness, and we were in love. I had a lovely passage. My love affair with the seas also began on that trip.

In the meantime, the storms took on epic proportion. I often found myself virtually alone on deck as, holding on to cables, with the sea spray on my face, I watched the silvery gray undulating waves of the Atlantic Ocean. The ship bobbed up and down, now and then catching a huge wave, then dropping with a loud crash onto its wake. I loved the wildness of it all. Evenings I learned from Frank about Brooklyn, his home, and the book *The Postman Always Rings Twice* ("Rip me again Frank," she said). I had a nice Serbian girl for a friend who also knew a crewmember, and the four of us would sit on the metal stairs chatting away half the night. Sometimes I became anxious that we would be found out, since fraternizing with the crew was not allowed. I even had a terrific panic attack one day. I was absolutely terrified as I imagined being sent back to Europe for my insubordination. The Serbian girl, who borrowed my blue winter coat with the fur collar, informed me on our last day that since she couldn't find me, she threw the coat overboard. Maybe she wasn't that nice. Our adventure finally came to an end as we sailed into New York Harbor and the Statue of Liberty came into our view one glorious morning.

While I was enjoying this beautiful sight, unbeknownst to me, my frantic parents were looking all over the ship for their lost daughter. My first experience on United States soil was a serious parental admonishment. It was at this point that Frank showed up to say a forlorn goodbye to me. We stood on a New York dock and my poor mother had to go through the whole dreaded routine again. She need not have worried. Within a week, her wayward daughter, the little weed, was safely enrolled in Central High School in Oklahoma City.

And so ends my story.

Epilogue

In the Spring of 1984, forty years after we left the old house, I returned to Budapest accompanied by my daughter, Veronika, and my husband, Daryl. I didn't just want to drop out of the sky into the city, so we flew to Vienna to get over our jet lag and then took the Orient Express from there. My cousin Mihaly and his wife, Agnes, picked us up at the station and after we settled in a hotel recommended by Uncle Aladar we finally arrived at the Old House where Uncle George, now eighty years old, was waiting for us with his two little grand-daughters Anna and Susan. We had two balmy spring days before the weather turned nasty. Agnes gave us tea and pastries under the old horse chestnut tree on the once manicured lawn now gone wild. We walked the eerily unchanged old neighborhood among the familiar villas with unkempt gardens. The one next door was now an orphanage and little children's faces looked at us from behind the window. A Russian soldier asked my husband not to take photographs and to put the cap back on his lens. Later we had a leisurely luncheon in the old dining room. I talked, laughed, listened and no one, not even I, suspected, what a profound effect the experience had on me. It was as though I were in a time warp—everything looked familiar yet it was not, and never became, the place I knew as my home. Not then nor ever again.

I hated our hotel—our phone was bugged. Every time I picked up the receiver a weird whistling sound came on before the dial tone. I found a green button from a hotel maid's uniform in the bottom of my suitcase. I fancied it was either a warning or a microphone, but it was probably just a curious person wanting to know what a rich American was wearing these days. I had a panic attack and took gobs of Valium before I could sleep. The next day we transferred to the airy Art Nouevau Gellert Hotel where Mommy and I went to her spa in the olden days. I was feeling much better and we went sight seeing and shopping and sat in sidewalk cafés. Nevertheless there was a somber atmosphere throughout the city. People on the street walked without expression and avoided all eye contact. The shopkeepers were brusque and sometimes downright rude.

One night Uncle George and I had a long telephone conversation. We talked mostly about my Mother. I told him that her husband once said to me that she really never loved anyone as much as her brother. Even over the telephone I could sense how much that effected him. The following evening we were expected for supper at the old house and we took the streetcar, still Number 83 as it was when I rode it every morning to school. Tearful faces welcomed us as we entered the foyer. Uncle George died of a massive heart attack the night before. For a long time afterwards I felt very bad for my behavior in the days that followed. I wondered if I should have stayed. But I had to get out. Mihaly and

Agnes came to the train station. It was cold and gray and the rain fell like tear drops from the sky but our eyes were dry. I was given a bouquet of lilies of the valley from the old garden. The mood was awful—I was running away again leaving others to the unpleasant tasks. Running away. Always running away. Then I wondered if I was the cause of it all. When I was finally able to verbalize some, though not all, of my concerns my husband reassured me "No, you didn't cause his death. Quite the contrary. Uncle George was probably waiting for you". Perhaps. I like to think he did.

My parents never went back to Hungary. Mommy maintained a close correspondence with the family and sent money and packages to them for many years. After my grandparents died, she seemed to be little more relaxed—not so worried anymore. She and George lived the last thirty plus years of their lives in Palo Alto California. George worked at Stanford University Law School. Mommy lived to be almost ninety. When the end was near we took turns sitting by her bed. One afternoon while watching her sleep, I had a sudden and fleeting sense that she was dying of her wounds from the war. On October 8, 1990, Mommy died.

The following summer I had an unexpected message on my answering machine. It was from my brother Zdenko whom I had not seen since he came to say goodbye in September of 1944. He had been to Budapest and got my phone number from Agnes and Mihaly. He was living in Toronto and he came to visit in August. Veronika joined us. I wish I could say we had a great visit with brotherly/sisterly love flowing all over the place. Perhaps we were too much alike; perhaps we both expected too much, albeit I felt a connection between us. We corresponded for the year, and he was planning a longer visit for next spring. I was looking forward to it as a chance for us to get closer to each other. Tragically during a routine physical examination it was discovered that he had an aggressive type of lymphoma. He chose to go for a radical treatment but he died the following October.

Since our first visit in 1984, I have been back to Hungary a few more times. Our last visit was in the spring of 2004—the atmosphere now was much more open and the people more friendly than during the oppressive Communist era. We visited a town in the southwest of the country where the Csontvary Museum is located. At one point during our visit someone asked me how old I was when I left the homeland in 1944. When I told him, the man turned, looked me over scrutinizingly, and put his two hands on the sides of my shoulders. "Madame" he said "you would not look this good had you stayed here".

The Old House now belongs to my cousin Mihaly and his ever- growing family. It is still lovely. Most of the furniture has been restored to its former beauty by his Agnes' diligence and talent. The paintings are still there too. I would like to have my Csontvary-Kostka pictures in my house but I never said so and, of course, nobody of the family offered them. I am only a visitor in that land. After all, it was I who made the decision to turn the key in the bathroom door.

It is now 2008. I am content these days. I love my daughter, my husband and my black Lab, and all is well with my world. But it is not all well with the world at large. Is it? I wrote a memoir primarily for my daughter and because so many people urged me to put my little stories on paper. In the end I wrote it for me really because it was fun. I think of it now not so much as a chronicle of what happened to me, although it is just that, but as a chronicle of what happens to people, even those who survive and later prosper, when their world is torn to bits by a war. When the Berlin wall came down my daughter rejoiced that the world had come its senses and peace had arrived. My mother gave her a sidelong glance: "Don't be too sure" she said.

Printed in the United States
139959LV00005B/4/P